MW01127386

"Many abused and neglected because they found that churches are unable or unwilling to protect them. In contrast, many sex offenders love to go to church because they know that weak policies and poor training give them the best chance to get away with their crimes. *The Child Safeguarding Policy Guide* is a comprehensive, concrete resource that will aid churches in keeping children safe, holding offenders accountable, and witnessing their commitment to care for the least of these."

> **Victor Vieth,** Senior Director & Founder, Gundersen National Child Protection Training Center

"Nobody relishes a good long talk about child abuse—especially at church. But any place where trusting children gather provides opportunities for the predator. That makes child abuse a necessary discussion for any ministry. This book provides expert advice and guidance for that conversation. I pray God will use it to bring protection to many young lives."

> **Paul O. Wendland,** President and Professor of New Testament Studies, Wisconsin Lutheran Seminary

"As his aunt, I have known Basyle Tchividjian since before he was born. I can attest to his strong Christian character, his great sense of fun, his love for his family, his commitment to awaken the church to the growing epidemic of child sexual abuse, and his passion to do something about it. He has my applause!"

> **Anne Graham Lotz,** Author; speaker; chairperson of the National Day of Prayer; Supporter of Grace; www.annegrahamlotz.org

"Simply put, *The Child Safeguarding Policy Guide* is now the standard for any ministry desiring to create safe and protected environments where the precious souls of children can flourish. This guide provides the direction needed to implement a complete care system that prevents abuse, as well as loving interventions for those affected when the unimaginable happens. I can't think of anyone more qualified than Boz and his team to write this groundbreaking guide."

> **Santiago "Jimmy" Mellado,** President and CEO, Compassion International

"*The Child Safeguarding Policy Guide* is a much-needed, beautifully-researched resource created for churches and ministries so that all children can be protected, heard, and healed in a predatory world. Every church should read this book and put its succinct and simple policies into practice."

Mary DeMuth, Author of over thirty books, including *Not Marked: Finding Hope and Healing after Sexual Abuse*

"Jesus said, 'Bring the children to me. . . .' This is the definitive guide for protecting those whom we are seeking to bring to him. Detailed, practical, specific, and with appropriate recognition of when and how exceptions may be made to 'gold standard policies,' *The Child Safeguarding Policy Guide* should be in every church and Christian school library in the world."

Samuel T. Logan, Associate International Director, The World Reformed Fellowship

"To be welcomed into a church is to be welcomed into the arms of God's people. It is meant to be a welcoming embrace of love. Any predatory threat to any person in that church tragically harms the whole church and poisons its capacity to embrace. Basyle Tchividjian has offered to the church an enormous gift by offering not only policies and guidelines for protecting children, but also teaching us on a subject too many have avoided. I am grateful for his thoroughness and his obvious pastor's heart. Christian leaders should take heed."

Greg Brewer, Bishop of the Episcopal Diocese of Central Florida

"*The Child Safeguarding Policy Guide* is a book every church pastor, staff member, teacher, youth worker, and women's ministry leader should read. Written by a team of child abuse experts, and coauthored by Basyle Tchividjian of GRACE, this book offers solid practical advice for keeping church children safe from sexual and other forms of abuse. It is a must read and I highly recommend this book."

Denise George, Author of over thirty books, including *What Pastors Wish Church Members Knew*

"Being a local church pastor for almost fifty years, I know of no better organization or system of safeguarding the children of our church than GRACE ministries. I have learned from and admired Boz for years. This amazing book gives every church the best equipping tool to protect our most precious congregants (our children) from the most heinous of acts."

Joel C. Hunter, Senior Pastor, Northland, A Church Distributed

"Child abuse is a fearful, uncomfortable, and shocking topic that some church leaders may want to ignore. But Jesus's ministers must run TOWARD the battle. We're called to disciple children to be worshipers of God—but you can't disciple an unsafe child. Safeguarding is a spiritual pursuit. Basyle Tchividjian and the GRACE team have crafted an invaluable resource to educate and guide church leaders in building a safe discipling environment for children. We've used this training at Thomas Road Baptist and will definitely utilize this guide with our team."

Matt Willmington, Director of Ministries, Thomas Road Baptist Church

"*The Child Safeguarding Policy Guide for Churches and Ministries* is a crucially important handbook for the protection of our children. Churches and faith communities should be one of the safest places for children to grow up, learn, and play. Tragically, this is not always the case. Basyle Tchividjian and Shira Berkovits bring not only their hearts to this mission but years of dedication and experience in this field.

This book is an answer to prayer for those who deeply desire to protect the children of their communities and who are seeking practical guidance in how to achieve this. Protecting our most vulnerable should always be of absolute importance for all of us. Amidst the untold suffering and silence, we hear the words of Christ in our hearts saying, 'Let the little children come to me and do not hinder them, for to such belongs the kingdom of heaven.'"

Jonathan Jackson, Star of CMT's *Nashville*; Lead singer of Enation; author of *The Mystery of Art*

"This book could save your ministry. As a seminary president, I am mindful of the insidious challenge of child sexual abuse in what should be the safest of places—church. Boz Tchividjian and G.R.A.C.E. have provided guidelines to help churches avoid such tragedies and if they occur, how to deal with them. *The Child Safeguarding Policy Guide* should be required reading for every pastor, church worker, and seminarian. As uncomfortable as this topic is, Christians cannot avoid it."

Frank A. James, President and Professor of Historical Theology, Biblical Theological Seminary

"Scripture tells us to 'speak up for those who cannot speak for themselves'—that has to include children! They have no more courageous a defender than my friend Boz, who is passionate about helping the church protect its children. Our good intentions are not enough. Use this excellent, comprehensive, and practical guide, developed by experts incorporating best-practice child protection policies and procedures, to help your church or ministry recognize, prevent and respond to child abuse. Make sure your environment is safe for innocent children and unsafe for those who would do them harm. A very important book!"

Wess Stafford, President Emeritus, Compassion International

"Forty-five years of counseling, writing, and speaking have shown me that the church is a powerful system—one meant by God to bend down as he did and care for least. I have also learned that powerful systems can easily be dangerous places for the small and the vulnerable. Sadly, the church has often protected abusers and itself, thus further traumatizing victims. *The Child Safeguarding Policy Guide*, coauthored by Basyle Tchividjian and Shira Berkovits, is the first book that provides the A to Z of developing comprehensive child protection policies. It is my prayer that the gift of this resource will transform the church, so she is known as a refuge for all.

Diane Langberg, Psychologist; author of *Suffering and the Heart of God*

"Some lessons are much too important for pastors not to grasp early on in their ministries. One such lesson is how to protect the most vulnerable souls in our churches, namely, the children. I know of no better teacher and mentor for church leaders on this subject than Boz Tchividjian. In *The Child Safeguarding Policy Guide*, Boz gives pastors, children's staff, and volunteers everything they need to protect children from having their souls vandalized by abuse. Please read this guide and, much more importantly, implement it as soon as possible in your ministry."

Scott Sauls, Senior pastor, Christ Presbyterian Church, Nashville, TN; author of *Befriend* and *From Weakness to Strength*

THE CHILD SAFEGUARDING POLICY GUIDE

....

FOR CHURCHES AND MINISTRIES

....

Basyle Tchividjian
and Shira M. Berkovits

New
Growth
Press

WWW.NEWGROWTHPRESS.COM

New Growth Press, Greensboro, NC 27404
Copyright © 2017 by GRACE

Unless otherwise indicated, Scripture quotations are taken from *The Holy Bible, English Standard Version.*® Copyright © 2000; 2001 by Crossway Bibles, a division of Good News Publishers. Used by permission. All rights reserved.

Scripture quotations marked NIV are taken from THE HOLY BIBLE, NEW INTERNATIONAL VERSION®, NIV® Copyright © 1973, 1978, 1984, 2011 by Biblica, Inc.® Used by permission. All rights reserved worldwide.

All Christian theological content contributed by Basyle Tchividjian

Cover Design: Faceout Books, faceoutstudio.com
Typesetting and eBook: Lisa Parnell, lparnell.com

ISBN 978-1-945270-05-5 (Print)
ISBN 978-1-945270-06-2 (eBook)

Library of Congress Cataloging-in-Publication Data
Names: Tchividjian, Basyle, author.
Title: The child safeguarding policy guide
    for churches and ministries / Basyle Tchividjian, Shira Berkovits.
Description: Greensboro, NC : New Growth Press, 2017. | Includes bibliographical references and index.
Identifiers: LCCN 2017012472 | ISBN 9781945270055 (print)
Subjects: LCSH: Church work with children. | Corporations, Religious—Safety measures. | Child abuse—Prevention. | Child abuse—Religious aspects—Christianity. | Child sexual abuse—Prevention. | Child sexual abuse—Religious aspects—Christianity.
Classification: LCC BV639.C4 T438 2013 | DDC 261.8/3271—dc23
LC record available at https://lccn.loc.gov/2017012472

Printed in the United States of America

24 23 22 21 20 19 18 17   1 2 3 4 5

CONTENTS

Policy Section Five: Living the Policy

GETTING STARTED
WITH CHILD SAFEGUARDING

Children are one of the greatest treasures any church holds. Imagine the joy children bring to a congregation: their laughter, their energy, their curiosity, their sincere faith. Jesus agrees. He said, "Whoever welcomes one of these little children in my name welcomes me; and whoever welcomes me does not welcome me but the one who sent me" (Mark 9:37 NIV). When our churches are full of children, Jesus is present. At Godly Response to Abuse in the Christian Environment (GRACE), we believe that our care of children—our "welcoming" of them among us—is a direct reflection of our love for and obedience to God. As the sweet nursery song teaches, Jesus loves the little children, and one of the most important works any church can undertake—to love God—is to love the children in its care.

The GRACE team who put this guide together believes in providing compassionate care and advocacy for children. Because you are reading this guide, we believe you do too.

The mission of GRACE is to empower the Christian community through education and training to recognize, prevent, and respond to child abuse. In the GRACE team's experience, we have met many sincere Christians who want to protect the children in their care and respond well if any harm ever came to these children, but they also know that doing so is easier said than done. People who harm children create and/or exploit whole environments that make child advocacy difficult. This guide offers support and help to those who want to overcome these challenging realities.[1]

Maybe the statistics about child sexual abuse and its prevalence alerted you to the problem. Maybe you have experienced or seen firsthand the harm any form of child maltreatment brings to precious souls. Whatever reason brought you to this guide, we hope you find it informative, healing, helpful, and encouraging. This guide is a way to partner with local churches, joining forces to protect children—an attainable goal. As psychologist Anna Salter says, "It is precisely our lack of knowledge and understanding that gives predators their edge, and there's nothing wrong with trying to level the playing field a little."[2]

Churches can level the playing field by cultivating a proactive culture of protection that prioritizes their children's safety. By taking the time to work through this guide and implement child safeguarding best practices, your church can work to prevent child sexual abuse and other forms of childhood maltreatment, and respond well when it occurs. The guide will walk you through developing and implementing a Child Protection Policy: the what, why, and how of child safeguarding within a local congregation.

Our prayer is that as you pursue child protection, you will also bring gospel light into the lives of the many adult survivors in your congregation and community. Many experts and survivors of child sexual abuse agree that an important way to demonstrate support to survivors is to enact and enforce child protection policies.

One survivor recounts how she avoided church for years until one day she felt God was telling her, "I didn't hurt you. It was evil men who used my name. It's time to come back." She ripped from her phone book the address of every church in her community. Working through the list, the woman drove to each church and asked the pastor to show her their child protection policy. If the pastor could not produce one, she moved on. If the pastor produced a poor policy, she walked away. After visiting more than twenty churches, she met a pastor who told her the church developed their policy working with local child protection professionals and that the policy was accompanied by annual training for all their workers. The church had reported cases of abuse, the pastor had preached against the sin of abuse, and the church was involved with community child abuse prevention programs. This was the church the woman chose—the church she found most welcoming to children who are hurting.

By reading and working through this guide, you are taking great strides to protect your children and care for anyone who carries the wounds of child abuse. Child abuse brings untold pain and suffering to the lives of real people, and shining a light into this dark topic is difficult but worth every effort.

Notes on How to Use This Guide:

The guide can be used alone, but it was originally developed as a part of the curriculum for GRACE's Child Safeguarding Certification. There may be times when you feel you need more help understanding a topic or navigating implementation. Pastors and church leaders often and understandably find themselves dealing with child safety issues that are out of their area of expertise. Being connected to the best resources in the field of child protection will greatly enhance your knowledge and support base. We encourage you to use the guide in conjunction with the Child Safeguarding Certification, where GRACE will connect your local church with one of its Certification Specialists, a real person who has extensive experience in child sexual abuse prevention and response. Through its Child Safeguarding Certification, GRACE provides additional, necessary resources and support.

Just as pastors and church leaders may need help from experts, they will also need help from within their congregations. Protecting children in a church is too much work for any one person, and one advocate for children is insufficient to sustain an environment of protection. We suggest that a Child Safeguarding Committee ("Committee") work through the guide together. Having a Committee will set up the church for long-term success—a culture where adults are educated and willing to protect kids. If you are a part of GRACE's Child Safeguarding Certification, your Certification Specialists will help you form a Committee. Appendix One also offers guidance on how to establish one.

While the guide and GRACE's Safeguarding Certification focus primarily upon child sexual abuse, where applicable, we will talk about other forms of child maltreatment: physical abuse, emotional abuse, neglect, and spiritual abuse. As will be discussed, when children are sexually abused, often they are abused in other ways as well. Similarly, protecting against one form of abuse can protect against others.

Throughout this guide you will also find numerous examples, illustrations, and stories. All of these are based on real incidents that have come across our desks, but details about the victims, perpetrators, and institutional settings (e.g., name, religious affiliation, gender, staff position) have been changed to protect the identities of those involved. In a number of instances, we have combined several cases into one, where we thought doing so would be more protective of the involved parties' identities.

Policy Section One

The Foundation

Adult-child relationships within the church bring untold benefits to the child, the adult, and the community. Children need adults in their lives—advising, loving, and shaping them in Christian faith. Adults pass down to children their community values, and nothing can replace rich, deep, multi-generational relationships for spiritual formation. Healthy communities promote healthy relationships. Understanding how child sexual abuse and other forms of child maltreatment work allows communities to pursue healthy behaviors and relationships because it allows them to competently identify abusive behaviors and relationships.

In one community, adults called a child-protection expert because they were concerned that two six-year-olds would wave and said "good day" to strangers as they passed by the church's playground. The community believed the children's behavior put them at risk for abuse. Waving hello to strangers with adequate adult supervision shows a beautiful hospitality, not an indication of danger. When protecting their children, some communities may want to protect their children against everything, even healthy behaviors and relationships. In doing so, they create a paranoid or fear-based culture instead of a proactive and protective culture.

And yet, to the other extreme, some communities miss abuse because they do not have a thorough definition and proper training. Common misconceptions still inform religious communities on child maltreatment. Maybe communities miss sexual abuse between

a teen and an adult, calling it "sexual activity" or an "inappropriate relationship"; maybe they believe that a child enjoyed the abuse
and thus is culpable in part; maybe they think that an adult who
touched a child's penis was *just touching*, with no long-term harm.
These communities may even be in denial about the prevalence of
child abuse and its impact. These dangerous misunderstandings
about abuse and abuse dynamics leave children unprotected.

The goal of a Child Protection Policy is to create a culture where
children can flourish with healthy intergenerational relationships,
including protecting them from maltreatment. But before a community can protect its children from child sexual abuse, they must
know what child sexual abuse is. Before communities can respond
appropriately to abused children, they must be able to spot indicators that children are being abused. Before communities can get
children who have been abused the help they need, they need to
know the impact of maltreatment. Finally, before communities
can curb abusive behavior, they must know how people who sexually abuse children behave. The following chapters explore these
dynamics of child sexual abuse and other forms of child maltreatment. They lay the foundation for proactive, protective measures.

CHAPTER ONE

. . . .

DEFINING ABUSE

With so many news reports and stories about child sexual abuse, defining it might feel intuitive, but communities who take this approach often fail children because they do not have an adequate understanding of it and other forms of child maltreatment. Instead of relying on popular (and possibly incorrect) definitions, the Child Protection Policy (henceforth, "Policy") can define child sexual abuse and child maltreatment for its community in a way that accounts for the community's legal obligations, the church's moral values, and current research.

A thorough Policy includes thorough definitions. Publicly defining child sexual abuse and child maltreatment may feel scary, but doing so will empower the community with knowledge that will allow it to take proactive, calm, preventative measures that protect the community, adults, and—most importantly—children. Clear definitions protect adults by giving them freedom to pursue healthy, loving relationships with children; they know what is acceptable behavior and what is not. Defining abuse also protects the church by ensuring the community complies with all its legal obligations. Each state has its own definition of abuse and for that matter, its own definition of child.[1] Search for your state's legal definition of child abuse and use it as a starting point. The Policy's definition of abuse must at least incorporate the state's definition.[2]

Nonetheless, while the behavioral requirements for criminal liability may be narrowly defined, actions that can damage a child are far less specific. For this reason, most churches will employ a broader definition of abuse, choosing to err on the side of protecting children even if such language encompasses behaviors that may or may not be illegal. In this respect, clear definitions protect children by accurately identifying harmful behavior as abusive and guiding the community toward healthy behaviors that allow children to flourish.

This guide focuses on preventing and responding to child sexual abuse because it is a serious threat to children. However, abuse rarely comes in only one form. Research indicates that children exposed to one form of maltreatment are often experiencing other forms of maltreatment. Sexual abuse often includes emotional and spiritual abuse. Physical abuse can involve bullying or sexual abuse. The term for this dynamic is polyvictimization because children often suffer many forms of victimization.

The Adverse Childhood Experiences (ACE) study surveyed adults about their childhood and asked adults whether, in their childhood, they had experienced[3] contact sexual abuse, physical abuse, emotional abuse, physical neglect, emotional neglect, a mother who was treated violently, a household member who used substances, a household member who was imprisoned, a household member who suffered from mental illness, and not being raised by both biological parents. Perhaps not surprisingly, researchers found that 66 percent of this sample had experienced at least one ACE category, and of those who did, 87 percent also experienced a second ACE category.

According to another study, 66 percent of maltreated children are abused in at least two ways, 30 percent are abused in at least 5 ways, and 10 percent endure 11 or more types of abuse.[4] This means that a child who suffers any form of abuse is often maltreated in other ways as well. One study found that children who had been physically assaulted in the past year were five times as likely to be sexually assaulted that same year.[5] Other studies have found that children from homes with familial dysfunction, such as parental discord, poor parent-child relationship, substance abuse, or physical or emotional unavailability, are at increased risk of sexual abuse.[6] Other conditions, such as a violent family or neighborhood and pre-existing emotional difficulties increase a child's likelihood of experiencing multiple types of maltreatment.[7] Finally, those who have been abused by one perpetrator are at increased risk of experiencing repeat maltreatment of the same kind by other perpetrators.[8]

Churches should use the knowledge of polyvictimization in their efforts to protect youth.

- When a child is identified as the victim of one type of mal-treatment (e.g., sexual abuse), steps should be taken to protect the child from further harm in other areas.
- Include education on multiple forms of child maltreatment in your church trainings.
- Provide support for caregivers of children who are at increased risk for polyvictimization.
- Pay particularly close attention to youths in vulnerable circum-stances (e.g., living in violent homes or neighborhoods or who are emotionally neglected) and during vulnerable times (transi-tions into grade and high schools).

Accordingly, when your church protects a child from sexual abuse, you are often protecting the child from additional forms of maltreatment such as physical abuse or neglect. Therefore, the fol-lowing chapter defines sexual abuse, but also other forms of child maltreatment, including physical abuse, emotional abuse, neglect, and spiritual abuse. The guide will mostly reference child sexual abuse, but when applicable, it will reference these other forms of child maltreatment.

Sexual Abuse

Any occurrence in which an adult engages a minor in sexual activity is abusive. Sexual activity between an adult and child is abusive regardless of whether the adult or the child is the initiator, whether the activity is forced or not, or whether the child understands that the activity is sexual in nature. Sexual activity between children can also be abusive, particularly if there is a significant disparity in age, development, or size; if one child is in a position of responsibility, trust, or power over the other; if one child is unconscious; or if coercion is used. Sexual activity may include but is not limited to:

Contact Behavior

- touching with any part of one's body another's genitalia, buttocks, breasts, or surrounding areas (e.g., thighs, stomach, lower back), except as necessary for caregiving (such as changing an infant's diaper) or medical purposes (such as administering an Epi Pen to a child's buttocks).
- using one's own genitalia, buttocks, breasts, or surrounding areas to touch another's body (e.g., rubbing one's penis against a child's back)
- kissing, masturbation, oral sex, vaginal, anal, or other orifice penetration by a penis, finger or other object
- exploiting a child by engaging the child in prostitution or the production of pornography

Non-contact Behavior

- sexual communication (whether verbal or written, including by telephone, text message, email, or social media)
- voyeurism (spying on private or intimate behaviors, such as those involving undressing, nudity, or sexual activity)
- exposure to pornography or other sexually explicit material
- exhibitionism (exposure of part or all of an adult's naked body)

- exposure of part or all of a child's naked body (except as necessary for caregiving or medical purposes)
- any activity intended to abuse, degrade, arouse, or gratify sexual desires
- instruction from an adult for a child to engage in sexual activity alone or with a third party.

The child protection field uses various terms to describe these dynamics: child molestation, rape, or abuse to name a few. This guide will consistently use the term child sexual abuse.[9]

Denial of abuse is one of the primary impediments toward its prevention. Child sexual abuse is not a new phenomenon; it cuts across socioeconomic status, geographic location, race, and religion. Including a definition in the church's Policy acknowledges that the issue exists. Furthermore, defining abuse in the Policy acknowledges that abuse can and does happen within the Christian community, even possibly within your church. The Policy should include a statement about abuse's prevalence.

Sixty-seven percent of all sexual abuse reported to law enforcement in the United States each year is perpetrated against children.[10] It is impossible to know the true prevalence of child sexual abuse since many victims never report their abuse and many studies use non-standard definitions and varying methods of data collection.[11] However, the ACE study estimated that approximately 1 in 4 women and 1 in 6 men were sexually abused before the age of eighteen.[12] These staggering estimates underscore the pervasiveness of child sexual abuse and make it likely that every reader of this guide knows someone who has been, or is currently, the victim of sexual abuse.

Physical Abuse

In all fifty states, it is a crime to physically assault anyone, including a child. Although definitions vary, generally a physical assault involves conduct intended to cause physical pain or injury. In many states, it is also unlawful to place anyone in fear of being assaulted.[13] Accordingly, kicking, punching, slapping, choking, throwing objects, or otherwise inflicting pain or fear of immediate injury to a child is unlawful and should be reported to law enforcement.

Although the law permits parents to use corporal punishment, the law requires the discipline to be reasonable.[14] Churches may be hesitant to address where the line is on corporal punishment for fear of offending parents. Parenting and discipline are understandably very personal and sensitive subjects. However, when churches name physically abusive actions, they can also help promote careful and thoughtful discussion about the Bible's teaching on discipline. Churches can promote the many biblical forms of discipline, including guidance, correction, and teaching. Furthermore, churches that name physical abuse guard against people who might misinterpret, misapply, or justify their abuse with the Bible. Pastors must challenge people who excuse any form of abusive behavior with justifications from the Bible.[15]

The Centers for Disease Control report that 28 percent of more than seventeen thousand respondents in the ACE study indicate that they were physically abused before the age of eighteen. These numbers only include abuse that was so forceful as to result in injury or lasting marks on the child. Further, unlike with sexual abuse, the prevalence of physical abuse provided in the ACE study is limited to abuse perpetrated by an adult living in the child's home and does not account for abuse perpetrated by those in positions of authority over the child outside the home (e.g., teachers or counselors) or by other children.[16] In a study of 4,549 children, the Department of Justice discovered that nearly one half of children surveyed were physically assaulted in the past year alone.[17] In another study, more than 1.25 million children were found to have been maltreated in the US alone in one year. Of those who had been abused, most had been physically abused.[18]

Think back to your own childhood in schools, camps, extracurricular programs and churches; chances are good that you can recall at least one staff member who was a little too physically aggressive and certainly a number of children who did not hesitate to beat up on a younger—or more vulnerable—child. One young boy seemed to always be the target of his teachers. Some would wrestle him to the ground, others would throw erasers and chalk when he asked one too many questions, and one particularly violent teacher threw a metal chair straight at his head. Such violence is not necessarily the exception or a relic of abusive educational practices that do not exist anymore. Recently, three young boys explained what they like most about their new school: the teachers do not beat them.

Emotional Abuse

Children suffer from emotional or psychological abuse when they are repeatedly ridiculed, blamed, humiliated, or compared unfavorably to others.[19] In some instances, an adult may verbally terrorize a child by threatening to beat, cut, or commit other atrocities. It is also possible to abuse a child emotionally through unrelenting pressure to meet impossible expectations in academics, athletics, or other areas. One child abuse prevention guide defines emotional abuse as "derogatory name-calling and put-downs or persistent and deliberate coldness from a person—to the extent where the behavior of the child is disturbed or their emotional development is at serious risk of being impaired. Serious emotional or psychological abuse could also result from conduct that exploits a child without necessarily being criminal, such as encouraging a child to engage in inappropriate or risky behaviours."[20]

The CDC estimates that more than 10 percent of children have been emotionally abused at home, with girls experiencing significantly higher rates of abuse than boys; these numbers do not account for the emotional abuse children experience outside the home or within the home from other children.[21] Often, the emotional abuse is blatant or overheard by others in an institution, but it is dismissed as merely uncomfortable, awkward, or mean.

Emotional abuse can stand alone, but it often accompanies other forms of child maltreatment. In one study, for example, emotional abuse was found to be present in the vast majority of physical abuse cases.[22] This can happen, for example, when an adult beats a child and says the beating is because the child is stupid or ugly or disobedient. In one case, a pastor sexually abused a five-year-old girl, but after several weeks of abuse, she resisted the pastor and shouted at him to leave her alone. The pastor quickly clamped his hand over her mouth and said, "You've ruined everything! You are the worst child in this entire church." Years later, the girl still struggles with feelings of inadequacy and a belief that she is at the core a "bad girl."

Emotional abuse can also involve bullying. Bullying[23] is defined as any form of harassment that one should reasonably expect would demean, threaten, or hurt (physically or emotionally). Bullying can be physical, verbal, demonstrative, or electronic. It can be of a sexual nature or otherwise. It can take place in person, over the phone, in cyberspace, or through an on-line communication, or any other means that communicates such harassment. It can be one-on-one or group-based. Both adults and children can be bullied or be the bully.

Neglect

In many cases, neglect involves depriving a child of food, clothing, shelter, medical care, education, or other necessities of life. Neglect can also involve exposing a child to harmful substances or practices such as drugs, alcohol, or violence. Sometimes neglect is emotional, such as when a parent completely ignores or rejects a child. Parents who cannot provide for children as a result of poverty are not committing neglect, though these parents and children may need assistance. Neglect, instead, is a deliberate act that impacts children physically and emotionally. In some instances, neglect can cost children their lives.

Neglect is the continued failure to provide a child with the basic necessities of life, such as food, clothing, shelter, hygiene, medical attention, or adequate supervision, to the extent that the child's health, safety, and/or development is, or is likely to be, jeopardized. Neglect can also occur if an adult fails to adequately ensure the safety of a child where the child is exposed to extremely dangerous or life-threatening situations.

Neglect may be:

- Physical (e.g., failure to provide necessary food or shelter, or lack of appropriate supervision)
- Medical (e.g., failure to provide necessary medical or mental health treatment)
- Educational (e.g., failure to educate a child or attend to special education needs)
- Emotional (e.g., inattention to a child's emotional needs, failure to provide psychological care, or permitting the child to use alcohol or other drugs)

Neglect is the most prevalent form of child maltreatment in the US,[24] but it is often overlooked in the institutional context. It is hard to imagine that parents in our community might starve their child, or that a youth director might feed all of the children on a weekend trip while neglecting to feed a specific child or a select group, but these things can and do happen.

Spiritual Abuse

An often-overlooked form of psychological maltreatment is the infliction of spiritual abuse on a child. According to dozens of studies involving more than nineteen thousand abused children, a large number of maltreated children have not only been injured physically and emotionally, but also spiritually.[25] Child spiritual abuse is abuse administered under the guise of religion. It includes harassment or humiliation and possibly results in psychological trauma or spiritual injuries. Spiritual abuse may include misuse of religion for selfish, secular, or ideological ends. Spiritual abuse can occur when a perpetrator incorporates religion into the abuse of a child. Examples of spiritual abuse include:

- Use of religious ideology, precepts, tradition, or sacred texts to harm a child
- Compelling a child to engage in religious acts against his or her will
- Abuse that occurs in a religious context (e.g., church)
- Abuse perpetuated by a religious leader (e.g., pastor)
- Invocation of divine authority to manipulate a child into meeting the needs of the abuser

In one case, a youth pastor who sexually abused a teenage girl in the church would do so in the church sanctuary. In her memoir, the girl explained that her abuser told her, "the love we shared was sacred, and so the sanctuary was the perfect place."[26] The youth pastor also told her that the sexual abuse he perpetrated on her was "God's will."[27] Messaging of this nature can be profoundly and spiritually damaging. In other cases, a spiritual injury may result because a child has unanswered questions. The child may have prayed that the abuse stop and wonders why a God who can part seas and raise the dead chooses not to stop beatings, rapes, starvation, and other atrocities.

According to a number of studies, children who have been spiritually injured are often angry with God, develop a fear of dying, leave their houses of worship and, in some instances, abandon their faith tradition altogether. This same research, though, finds that when faith communities assist children in healing from spiritual injuries, these children also do a better job of coping emotionally and spiritually.[28]

Policy Worksheet: Defining Abuse

What is your state's legal definition of "child"?_____

_____

_____

For the purposes of your Policy, how will you define a child? ____

_____

_____

Consider whether you will you use the legal definition for your Policy, or extend the law to apply to older children (e.g., up to twenty-one years old) as well.

Sexual Abuse

What is your state's legal definition of "child sexual abuse"? _____

_____

_____

Are there any ideas or words missing from the legal definition that you want to include in your Policy? If so, what are they? _____

_____

_____

This guide defines sexual abuse as physical contact with a sexual or intimate part of the body, or other forms of sexual activity, conducted without consent, or engaged in for the purpose of sexual gratification or to degrade or abuse.[29]

Physical contact includes:

» Touching, grabbing, patting, slapping, pinching, rubbing, fondling, groping, poking, or other forms of contact, whether over or under clothing

» Rubbing one's genital area up against another person or touching another person with one's genitals, whether over or under clothing. This includes instances when an individual acts as though the rubbing was inadvertent but was in fact intentional.

» Sexual intercourse of any kind

Sexual or intimate body parts include, but are not limited to:

» Breasts
» Buttocks
» Genitals
» Groin area
» Upper thighs

Other forms of sexual activity include:

» Photographing, videotaping, or making any other visual, descriptive, or auditory recording of sexual activity or the sexual or intimate parts of a person's body

» Displaying to another any writings, photograph, videotape, or other visual or auditory recording of sexual activity or the sexual or intimate parts of a person's body

Lack of consent includes:

» Explicit indication of lack of consent
» Physical/verbal force or intimidation, whether express or implicit
» Circumstances making it obvious that consent has not been granted, such as:

- ~ If one individual is an adult and one individual is a child, since children cannot legally consent to sexual activity with an adult.
- ~ Being too intoxicated to say "no"
- ~ Being asleep
- ~ Lack of knowledge of the activity's occurrence
- ~ Otherwise not having the physical or mental capacity to consent.

Underline the language you will include in your Policy.

Your Sexual Abuse Definition: _____

_____

_____

Physical Abuse

What is your state's legal definition of "child physical abuse"? ___

_____

_____

Are there any ideas or words missing from the legal definition that you want to include in your Policy? If so, what are they? _____

_____

_____

The guide defines physical abuse as a non-accidental physical injury (ranging from minor bruises to severe fractures or death) as a result of punching, beating, kicking, biting, shaking, throwing, stabbing, choking, hitting (with a hand, stick, strap, or other object), burning, or otherwise harming a child, that is inflicted by a parent, caregiver, or other person who has responsibility for the child. Such injury is considered abuse regardless of whether the caregiver intended to hurt the child. Physical discipline, such as spanking or paddling, is not considered abuse as long as it is reasonable and causes no bodily injury to the child.[30]

Underline the parts of the guide's definition you would like to include in your Policy.

Your Physical Abuse Definition: _____

_____

_____

Emotional Abuse

What is your state's legal definition of "child emotional abuse"? _

_____

_____

Are there any ideas or words missing from the legal definition that you want to include in your Policy? If so, what are they? _____

_____

_____

The Guide defines emotional abuse as acts toward a child that cause or have a substantial likelihood of causing harm to the child's physical, psychological, social, spiritual, or moral development. Emotional abuse might include, but is not limited to, patterns of:

- » restricting a child's movement
- » discrimination (e.g., serving snack to all the children in a youth group except for one child or one group of children)
- » blaming
- » belittling, denigrating, ridiculing, or humiliating
- » threatening or scaring
- » unrealistic expectations and demands
- » other non-physical forms of hostility or bullying

Underline all parts of the Guide's definition that you would like to include in your Policy.

Your Emotional Abuse Definition: _____

_____

_____

Neglect

What is your state's legal definition of "neglect"? _____

_____

_____

Are there any ideas or words missing from the legal definition that you want to include in your Policy? If so, what are they? _____

_____

_____

> » Physical (e.g., failure to provide necessary food or shelter, or lack of appropriate supervision)
> » Medical (e.g., failure to provide necessary medical or mental health treatment)
> » Educational (e.g., failure to educate a child or attend to special education needs)
> » Emotional (e.g., inattention to a child's emotional needs, failure to provide psychological care, or permitting the child to use alcohol or other drugs)

Your Neglect Definition: _____

_____

_____

Spiritual Abuse

The guide defines child spiritual abuse as abuse administered under the guise of religion.

Examples include:

» Use of religious ideology, precepts, tradition, or sacred texts to harm a child
» Compelling a child to engage in religious acts against his or her will
» Abuse that occurs in a religious context (e.g., church)
» Abuse perpetuated by a religious leader (e.g., pastor)
» Invocation of divine authority to manipulate a child into meeting the needs of the abuser

Place a check mark by any of the examples you will include in your Policy's definition.

Your Spiritual Abuse Definition: _____

_____

_____

Sample Policy Language:

[Faith Church][31] takes all indicators and suspicions of child maltreatment seriously. We are aware of the research on polyvictimization, which tells us that children who are maltreated in one way are at significantly increased risk of being maltreated in multiple ways. Therefore, as our church becomes aware of an indicator or report of a child being maltreated in one way, we will be alert to the possibility that this child might also be maltreated in another way, and we will take steps to protect the child from known risks and be extra attentive to and supportive of the child.

CHAPTER TWO

· · · ·

INDICATORS

By understanding some of the behaviors that might indicate a child is being sexually abused, churches are in a better position to intervene to help the child. Often, children who are being abused exhibit difficult behaviors, making it unlikely that these children will be believed if they disclose. So often, people protest an abuse disclosure because of who the child is. "Who, that child?" they might say. "You have to take everything she says with a grain of salt; you can't imagine how troubled she is." Or, "That family? They are always complaining about something and stirring up trouble. The man they've accused, on the other hand—he has a sterling reputation." If only these individuals understood that this is exactly the response the child's abuser anticipated.

Child victims often come to the community's attention as adolescents or young adults involved in risky or criminal behaviors. The community may insist on seeing these children as delinquent, but there is another option. Rather than labeling children, communities can recognize that they may be witnessing the consequences of child sexual abuse or another form of maltreatment in a vulnerable child's life. For the sake of the tens of thousands of children who silently suffer sexual abuse each year, churches must educate themselves and create policies that acknowledge indicators of abuse so that they can then respond appropriately.

Henry's Story, Part One

Henry, a six-year-old boy from a large city, wanted to attend his church's summer day camp for as long as he could remember. The camp was expensive and Henry's young parents were struggling to make ends meet. They met with the camp director who successfully secured them a scholarship. Henry could barely contain his excitement throughout the first week of camp, but in the coming weeks, Henry's parents saw their previously fun-loving and respectful son become surly and unhappy.

By the second week, Henry's parents noted a change in his behavior and affect. The normally animated boy became sullen and withdrawn. Where Henry was usually respectful and helpful at home, he became belligerent. His parents asked if anyone was bothering him at camp, but Henry refused to talk about it. Henry began complaining of nausea and picking morosely at his food, barely eating. When his mother asked him about his week, Henry responded, "It was awful!" Pressed to elaborate, he explained that he had been forced to sit by the camp director during lunch and said, "He's ugly and smells bad!"

By the third week, Henry was rapidly losing weight and had a constant pale, drawn expression. Despite his parents' increased support and attention, Henry began to vomit daily and use his toys to self-harm. Eventually, Henry refused to go back to camp. Henry's parents knew something was off with their son, and they set out to explore what could be at the root of his behavior.

Indicators of Child Sexual Abuse

Sometimes the explanation for a child's different behavior is innocent, and sometimes it is worrisome. But in all cases, stress indicators are a signal that a child is struggling with something and may be in need of help. Below, behavioral and emotional indicators of child sexual abuse are listed. No indicator on its own is conclusive of child sexual abuse; in fact, most reflect injuries or behaviors that non-abused, typically developing children may experience during childhood. However, indicators that are egregious, observed on multiple occurrences, or occur in conjunction with other indicators warrant careful inquiry and concern.

Possible Behavioral and Emotional Indicators[1]

Because a child's behavior may vary as the result of numerous factors unrelated to sexual abuse, behavioral indicators are less reliable markers than physical indicators; however, behavioral indicators are far more likely to be observed than are physical indicators. When observing changes in behavior, note the frequency and pattern of the new behavior, while simultaneously considering children's developmental age and any new changes in their environment (e.g., a young child may revert to bed-wetting after experiencing a major life transition such as the birth of a new sibling). Also, consider the possibility of other forms of maltreatment, such as physical abuse, emotional abuse, neglect, or spiritual abuse. Emotional or behavioral signs of child sexual abuse may include:

- Depression, emotionless or passive behavior, withdrawal from family, friends, church, or school; exhibiting low self-esteem or self-loathing
- Lack of attachment to a caregiver; displaying distrust or wariness at the approach of adults, caregivers, or specific people; fear of going home that may manifest by arriving at youth groups early, staying late, and appearing frightened or upset when it is time to return home
- Being constantly watchful, as though preparing for something bad to happen
- Sudden changes in behavior, including academic changes
- Extremes in behavior, such as over-compliance, overachieving or demanding behavior, extreme passivity, or behaving more responsibly than would be expected of a child that age

- Aggressive, destructive (e.g., fire-setting), demanding, or disruptive behavior; frequent and inexplicable anger, rebellion, or running away
- Self-degradation; self-injury (e.g., "cutting") or wearing long sleeves on hot days (to hide bruising or other injuries); Suicide attempts
- Delays in emotional, cognitive, physical, or academic development
- Unwillingness to change for or participate in certain youth department activities such as a gym night or swim program[2]
- Being inappropriately adult (e.g., parenting other children) or infantile (e.g., rocking or head-banging)
- Bed-wetting in children who have previously outgrown it; nightmares; difficulty sleeping
- Exhibiting high anxiety, including through physical problems associated with anxiety, such as chronic stomach pain or headaches
- Frequent, unexplained absences at school

Sex play between children of similar ages is often the result of a healthy, age-appropriate curiosity, but atypical sexual behavior in young children is concerning. Dr. William Friedrich of the Mayo clinic conducted a study of sexual behavior in children and found that it is normal for two-year-old children to be relatively sexual (compared to ten- to twelve-year-olds) and to become increasingly sexual until age five.[3] Some sex play, though, is atypical even for young children and may be indicative of sexual abuse. In order to identify concerning sex play, it is important to understand which sex play is normal. As with other indicators of abuse, if a child is observed engaging in concerning behavior, remain calm but seek guidance from a trained professional (e.g., pediatrician, mental health professional, Child Advocacy Center, GRACE Certification Specialist).

It is normal for a young child to engage in the following sexual behaviors:[4]

- Touching their genitals or masturbating
- Showing others their genitals (e.g., "I'll show you mine if you show me yours")
- Playing house or doctor
- Showing interest in bathroom functions
- Using dirty language for bathroom functions

It is atypical for a young child to engage in the following sexual behaviors:

- Placing mouth on sex part
- Asking others to engage in sexual acts
- Trying to have intercourse or imitating intercourse
- Undressing others, especially if done forcefully
- Imitating sexual positions with dolls
- Inserting an object into vagina or anus, especially if child continues to do so despite pain
- Manually stimulating or having oral or genital contact with pets
- Making sexual sounds
- Inserting tongue in mouth when kissing

Possible Physical Indicators

Physical signs of sexual abuse are uncommon, so when they are present they are cause for concern. Like all indicators of child maltreatment, physical indicators of sexual abuse do not mean that abuse has occurred, as each indicator could have causes unrelated to abuse. Urinary tract infections can be caused by a child "holding in" urine. Pregnancy can be the result of consensual sexual activity between two children. Injuries to the genitals can be caused by falling into or bumping up against a large object. Chapter Ten will walk you through how to report indicators of sexual abuse to the legal authorities, but before indicators can be reported, they must be recognized.

Possible indicators of sexual abuse include:

- Torn, stained, or bloody underclothing
- Difficulty, pain, or blood in the genital area when walking, sitting, or using the bathroom
- Discharge from the penis or vagina
- Injuries (e.g., bruises, tearing, bleeding), itching, or swelling in the genital, vaginal, or anal area
- Urinary tract infections, yeast infections, sexually transmitted diseases
- Promiscuity and early sexual activity
- Pregnancy

Indicators of Physical Abuse

Since all children get cuts and bruises that result from normal childhood activity, you may wonder what injuries, if any, are suspicious of physical abuse. In addressing this, it is helpful to remember that children are typically forward moving, frontal explorers. At a very young age, children develop a "parachute" reflex in which hands instinctively move forward to brace themselves from a fall. Accordingly, typical accidental injuries are to the front, bony parts of the body including hands, knees, shins, and elbows.

When, however, children are physically abused, blows may be administered to the head, buttocks, or legs. Sometimes, children can be hit so hard that a hand, or portions of a hand, can be imprinted on their face. Punches to a stomach may result in abdominal bruises. Even if there is no mark to the exterior, when children complain of pain or indicate they were punched in the stomach, such an allegation should be taken very seriously given the possibility of significant internal damage.

Injuries behind the ear, whip marks to backs or legs, ligature marks around wrists or ankles, or burns are often telltale signs of physical abuse. When children are being hit, they sometimes have defensive wounds as they try to shield their bodies or otherwise attempt to protect themselves or others. Marks on their hands, forearms, or back of the legs are indicative of defensive wounds. The following diagrams illustrate injuries that are suspicious of physical abuse.

WOUND IDENTIFICATION

Look for...Overall Body Cleanliness

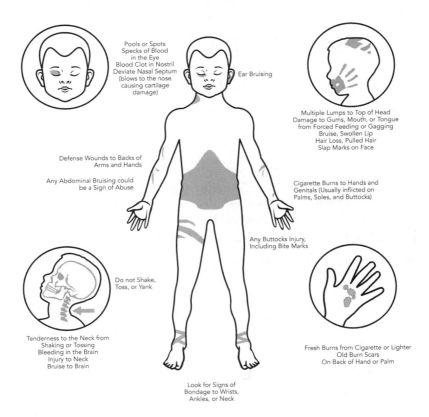

Pools or Spots
Specks of Blood
in the Eye
Blood Clot in Nostrum
Deviate Nasal Septum
(blows to the nose
causing cartilage
damage)

Ear Bruising

Multiple Lumps to Top of Head
Damage to Gums, Mouth, or Tongue
from Forced Feeding or Gagging
Bruise, Swollen Lip
Hair Loss, Pulled Hair
Slap Marks on Face

Defense Wounds to Backs of
Arms and Hands

Any Abdominal Bruising could
be a Sign of Abuse

Cigarette Burns to Hands and
Genitals (Usually inflicted on
Palms, Soles, and Buttocks)

Any Buttocks Injury,
Including Bite Marks

Do not Shake,
Toss, or Yank

Tenderness to the Neck from
Shaking or Tossing
Bleeding in the Brain
Injury to Neck
Bruise to Brain

Fresh Burns from Cigarette or Lighter
Old Burn Scars
On Back of Hand or Palm

Look for Signs of
Bondage to Wrists,
Ankles, or Neck

*Adapted from images designed by and provided courtesy of
the Youth Protection program of the Boy Scouts of America.

Look for Patterns such as
Belt Marks, Electrical Cord Marks

WOUND IDENTIFICATION

Look for...Overall Body Cleanliness

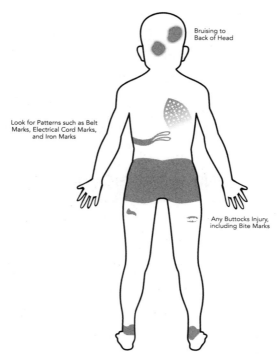

*Adapted from images designed by and provided courtesy of the Youth Protection program of the Boy Scouts of America.

Although children can break their bones through falls, sports, or other activities, some broken bones are commonly present in cases of child abuse. The diagram below illustrates injuries often present in cases of physical abuse.

MOST COMMON CHILD ABUSE FRACTURES

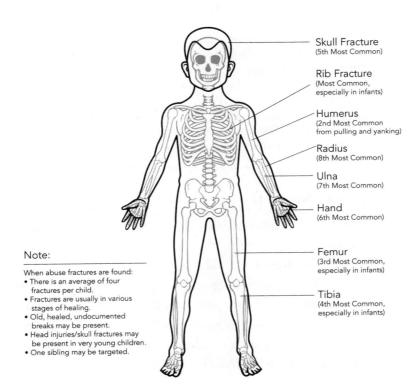

Skull Fracture
(5th Most Common)

Rib Fracture
(Most Common,
especially in infants)

Humerus
(2nd Most Common
from pulling and yanking)

Radius
(8th Most Common)

Ulna
(7th Most Common)

Hand
(6th Most Common)

Femur
(3rd Most Common,
especially in infants)

Tibia
(4th Most Common,
especially in infants)

Note:

When abuse fractures are found:
- There is an average of four
  fractures per child.
- Fractures are usually in various
  stages of healing.
- Old, healed, undocumented
  breaks may be present.
- Head injuries/skull fractures may
  be present in very young children.
- One sibling may be targeted.

*Adapted from images designed by and provided courtesy of
the Youth Protection program of the Boy Scouts of America.

Possible indicators of physical abuse include:

- Frequent injuries of any kind (e.g., bruises, cuts, fractures, burns)
- Especially if the child is unable to provide an adequate explanation of the cause of injury
- These injuries may appear in distinctive patterns such as grab marks, human bite marks, cigarette burns, or impressions of other instruments
- Pay particular attention to injuries that present on both sides of the head or body, as accidental injuries typically only affect one side of the body

Indicators of Neglect

There may be any number of clues that a child may be neglected. The child who always comes to church with a body odor; the child who is always unkempt; the child who is thrown out of his home; the child who is living in a dangerous environment; the child with an obvious medical need that goes unattended; the child who is always hungry, who hoards or steals food; the child who is never dressed appropriately for the weather; the child who references parents who are drunk on the couch—all of these may be signs of neglect.

Since no list is exhaustive of all the ways in which a child can be neglected, it may be helpful to follow a simple rule: anytime you encounter a child with a need or condition that a reasonable parent would attend to, the child may be neglected—especially if the need or condition is commonly observed. Take special note when the failure to provide the need will impair the child's physical or emotional well-being.

Consider the possibility of neglect if a child:

- Is obviously malnourished, listless, or fatigued
- Begs, steals, or hoards food or complains frequently of hunger
- Is consistently dirty or has a severe body odor
- Lacks sufficient clothing for the weather
- Has an untreated illness, injuries, health (e.g., unfilled cavities) or serious unmet educational needs
- Has broken or missing eyeglasses, hearing aid, or other necessary aids or equipment
- Has an untreated need for glasses, dental care, or other medical attention
- Stays at school outside of school hours
- Is frequently absent or has significant academic struggles
- Is inappropriately left unsupervised
- Abuses alcohol or other drugs

Indicators are a signal to pay attention and ask more questions. As with all indicators of child maltreatment, there are numerous explanations for each indicator of neglect that do not include neglect: A child who struggles academically may have an undiagnosed learning disorder. A child who comes to school in the winter without a coat may have forgetfully left it on the bus. Often an indicator of abuse or neglect ends up pointing to an issue completely unrelated to maltreatment (e.g., poverty), but one that requires a swift response nonetheless (e.g., governmental assistance). Familiarizing yourself with the indicators of neglect makes it more likely that you will understand the potential significance of what you are seeing and follow up with exploratory questions or actions.

Henry's Story, Part Two

When adults see an indicator of abuse, especially extreme or consistently repeated indicators, they must take action to find the source of the child's behavior. In Henry's case, his parents invested time and effort to discover what happened.

Henry's parents learned that his best-camp-friend, Shane, had been expelled from camp for shaking and kicking children at the bus stop and making sexually violent threats. When a neighbor mentioned Shane's expulsion to Henry, he became terrified and ran to his room. The next morning at breakfast, Henry told his parents that he could not sleep because he kept having nightmares about the camp director taking off his underwear and standing in front of him naked. His parents carefully asked, "Are these dreams?" Henry responded tentatively, "Well, I'm not asleep when I have these nightmares."

A CPS investigation determined that the camp director had sexually abused Shane, and that Henry had walked in on the abuse. For the rest of the summer, the camp director physically threatened Henry to remain silent, and made him witness Shane's ongoing abuse, convincing Henry that he was complicit in harming his friend. Months later, Henry disclosed his own abuse by the camp director, but only in bits and pieces. The extent of what Henry was made to suffer is still unclear. Because Henry's parents observed and explored his indicators of abuse, they figured out what happened to their son and were able to get him the help he needed. Faith communities can do the same for children in their care who exhibit these indicators.

Policy Worksheet:
Indicators of Child Sexual Abuse and Child Maltreatment

Sample Policy Language:

Because "the majority of children who are sexually abused will be moderately to severely symptomatic at some point in their life,"[5] [Faith Church] is familiar with and attentive to potential indicators of child sexual abuse. As the church's front-line for children's and youth programming and pastoral counseling, church professionals and volunteers have regular opportunities to observe children's behavior, family dynamics, and care-giving styles. They are often privy to the intimate details of congregants' lives. Unlike formal educators, church professionals have ongoing contact with the entire family unit and its acquaintances, and as such may be in the unique position to detect child sexual abuse and other forms of child maltreatment.

Underline the language you will include in your Policy. What would you add for your church's context? _____

_____

_____

The guide lists the following as indicators of child sexual abuse. Would you like to include specific indicators in your church's Policy?

_____ yes _____ no

If yes, check all that you will include in your Policy.

Consider the possibility of sexual abuse if a child has:

> » Torn, stained, or bloody underclothing
> » Difficulty, pain, or blood in the genital area when walking, sitting, or using the bathroom
> » Discharge from the penis or vagina
> » Injuries (e.g., bruises, tearing, bleeding), itching, or swelling in the genital, vaginal, or anal area
> » Urinary tract infections, yeast infections, sexually transmitted diseases
> » Pregnancy

It is atypical for children to engage in the following sexual behaviors:

> » Placing mouth on sex part
> » Asking others to engage in sexual acts
> » Trying to have intercourse or imitating intercourse
> » Undressing others, especially if done forcefully
> » Imitating sexual positions with dolls
> » Inserting an object into vagina or anus, especially if child continues to do so despite pain
> » Manually stimulating or having oral or genital contact with pets
> » Making sexual sounds
> » Inserting tongue in mouth when kissing

Emotional or behavioral signs of child sexual abuse may include:

> » Depression; emotionless or passive behavior; withdrawal from family, friends, church, or school; exhibiting low self-esteem or self-loathing
> » Lack of attachment to a caregiver; displaying distrust or wariness at the approach of adults, caregivers, or specific people; fear of going home that may manifest by arriving

at youth groups early, staying late, and appearing frightened or upset when it is time to return home

» Being constantly watchful, as though preparing for something bad to happen

» Sudden changes in behavior, including academic changes

» Extremes in behavior, such as over-compliance, over-achieving or demanding behavior, extreme passivity, or behaving more responsibly than would be expected of a child that age

» Aggressive, destructive (e.g., fire-setting), demanding, or disruptive behavior; frequent and inexplicable anger, rebellion, or running away

» Self-degradation; self-injury (e.g., "cutting") or wearing long sleeves on hot days (to hide bruising or other injuries); suicide attempts

» Delays in emotional, cognitive, physical, or academic development

» Unwillingness to change for or participate in certain youth department activities such as a gym night or swim program

» Being inappropriately adult (e.g., parenting other children) or infantile (e.g., rocking or head-banging)

» Bed-wetting in children who have previously outgrown it; nightmares; difficulty sleeping

» Exhibiting high anxiety, including through physical problems associated with anxiety, such as chronic stomach pain or headaches

» Frequent, unexplained absences at school

Consider the possibility of physical abuse if you notice:

» Frequent injuries of any kind (e.g., bruises, cuts, fractures, burns)

» Especially if the child is unable to provide an adequate explanation of the cause of injury

» These injuries may appear in distinctive patterns such as grab marks, human bite marks, cigarette burns, or impressions of other instruments
» Pay particular attention to injuries that present on both sides of the head or body, as accidental injuries typically only affect one side of the body

Consider the possibility of neglect if a child:

» Is obviously malnourished, listless, or fatigued
» Begs, steals, or hoards food or complains frequently of hunger
» Is consistently dirty or has severe body odor
» Lacks sufficient clothing for the weather
» Untreated illness, injuries, health (e.g., unfilled cavities) or serious educational needs
» Broken or missing eyeglasses, hearing aid, or other necessary aids or equipment
» Has an untreated need for glasses, dental care, or other medical attention
» Stays at school outside of school hours
» Frequently absent or significant academic struggles
» Is inappropriately left unsupervised
» Abuses alcohol or other drugs

CHAPTER THREE

. . . .

IMPACT

One man, a retired English teacher, lost his home and now lives on the streets in the frigid, snowy weather. Despite his harsh circumstances, he maintains a tremendous optimism, deep faith, and can-do spirit. However, as he was recounting how he had been sexually abused as a child, this man cried and told of how he felt broken inside. He has gone through unthinkable hardship in the past two years of his homelessness. Yet his childhood sexual abuse—that happened over sixty years ago—continues to cause him such pain. The biting wind, the empty stomach, and the abuse of strangers on the street have not touched his spirit, but the abuse of his innocence by someone who was supposed to protect him haunts him still. Many victims have similar experiences to this man's. Their maltreatment, far from being a mild childhood event, overshadows their life even into adulthood.

Children's souls are like wet cement. Child sexual abuse that occurs in a person's early years leaves an imprint that hardens. The imprint can be worn down over time, built upon if necessary, but never erased. Because child sexual abuse rarely results in observable physical injury, many believe that maltreatment—especially sexual or emotional abuse—is not such a big deal, and that children and adults should be able to *just get over it*.

Though a child's injuries may be hidden from the untrained eye, child sexual abuse can result in immediate and/or lasting impact in all realms of the person's well-being.[1] Understanding how child sexual abuse can traumatize the child and have lasting impact in the life of a surviving adult is a critical first step in preventing abuse and responding compassionately. Your church's Policy should include a statement that identifies the impact of child sexual abuse and other forms of child maltreatment. Not every child will display the impact of their maltreatment and not every adult will experience the long-term consequences of their traumatic childhood experiences, but all are at increased risk.

Impact on Emotional Health

It has long been known that maltreatment has immediate and long-term impact on a child's emotional, behavioral, and psychiatric health.[2] Furthermore, victims often say that the trauma from the communal response—shunning, shaming, disbelief—is worse than the trauma of the abuse itself. Statistical analyses of data from the ACE study found that children who had suffered one of the ten adverse childhood experiences surveyed[3] were at an increased risk throughout their lifetime for:[4]

- obesity
- smoking
- illicit drug use
- alcohol abuse
- marrying an alcoholic spouse
- early initiation of sexual activity
- unintended or teen pregnancies
- sexually transmitted diseases
- anxiety disorder
- depression

- attempting suicide
- experiencing domestic or sexual violence
- difficulties with academics, employment, or relationships
- hallucinations
- memory disturbances
- sleep disturbances

Sharon's Story

Consider the case of Sharon, a forty-four-year-old woman who was sexually abused in a church when she was nine years old. To this day, Sharon does not know the name of the congregant who abused her, but she remembers clearly what he did. On the outside, Sharon appears to be a confident businesswoman, social butterfly, and doting mother. But inside, Sharon feels as though she is falling apart. Since graduating college, Sharon has struggled with an eating disorder, depression, anxiety, and suicidal ideation. She has nightmares of her abuse at night and does not feel safe enough to sleep, despite having a loving and supportive husband. Sharon reports thinking about her abuse on a daily basis and feels as though one day she might just explode. Decades later, she still suffers at the hand of her abuser.

Impact on Physical Health

Child sexual abuse and child maltreatment have lasting physical impact as well as emotional.[5] Researchers analyzing data from the ACE study found that children who had experienced maltreatment were more likely to suffer from a variety of serious medical problems, including cancer, heart disease, lung disease, liver disease, autoimmune deficiencies, hypertension, diabetes, asthma, and obesity as adults.[6] These findings are astounding.

One possible explanation for the correlation is that victims of childhood maltreatment turn to coping behaviors (e.g., smoking, substance abuse, and overeating) in an attempt to manage the psychological symptoms of their maltreatment, and that these behaviors place them at direct risk for developing associated diseases (e.g., cancer, liver diseases, and diabetes). While this explanation is substantiated by research, ACE investigators found that it is only part of the story. The correlation between adverse childhood experiences and disease suggests that the maltreatment itself results in chronic stress that impacts the body's arousal system in a way that is not yet sufficiently understood.[7]

Impact on Spiritual Health

Children who have been maltreated often suffer immediate and long-term spiritual injuries in addition to their physical and emotional ones. A spiritual injury is an adverse impact on a child's relationship to God, religion, or spiritual well-being. Understanding the spiritual impact of maltreatment on the child victim and adult survivor is critical for pastors and church leaders who seek to create a spiritually safe and healthy religious environment for all congregants.

Spiritual injuries might include negative shifts in victims' perception of God (e.g., perceiving God as cruel, unfair, punitive, and distant), a ruptured relationship with God (e.g., feeling unloved by God), disruptions of faith (e.g., doubting God's existence), decreased involvement in organized religion (e.g., less willing to attend formal religious events), and a decline in spiritual well-being and functioning (e.g., feeling angry, guilty, or disconnected from one's sense of personal spirituality).[8] Children who have suffered sexual abuse often endure spiritual injury and may feel guilty, doubtful of God's existence, or believe that God is unjust.[9] In other cases, a spiritual injury may result because a child has unanswered questions.

When a child's abuser is religious or a member of the clergy, the abuser often uses religion to justify the molestation and communicates these distortions to the child.[10] Many abusers self-report the use of spiritual themes or cognitive distortions in their offending.

Victims report a sense of enhanced betrayal when their abuser is a person they perceived as holy, and numerous studies have found that spiritual injuries are more pronounced in instances when the perpetrator is a member of the clergy.[11]

James's Story

In one case that went to trial, a young child who had been sexually abused by a fellow church member describes the relief he felt when he saw the courtroom fill with the familiar and support-ive faces of his congregation. It was only when the judge called a recess and the congregants vocalized their support of the defen-dant that the child realized they were there in support of his abuser, and he felt the full impact of their betrayal. It should come as no surprise that this victim—now a grown adult—states that he cannot bear anything associated with religion. Had James's pastor taken a public stand to support him—an innocent child—the pastor could have helped James begin the healing process, instead of facilitating his re-victimization by the community.

Policy Worksheet: Impact of Child Sexual Abuse

Optional Policy Language:

> Though a child's injuries may be hidden from the untrained eye, child sexual abuse and other forms of child maltreatment can result in immediate and/or lasting impact in all realms of the person's well-being. Understanding how child sexual abuse can traumatize the child and have lasting impact in the life of a surviving adult is a critical first step in preventing abuse and responding compassionately. Not every child will display the impact of their maltreatment and not every adult will experience the long-term consequences of their traumatic childhood experiences, but all are at increased risk.

Would your church like to include more examples of impact? _____ yes _____ no

If yes, consider the following. Underline what you will include in your church's Policy.

Impact on Emotional Health

The ACE study found that children who had suffered one of the ten adverse childhood experiences surveyed were at an increased risk throughout their lifetime for: obesity, smoking, illicit drug use, alcohol abuse, marrying an alcoholic spouse, early initiation of sexual activity, unintended or teen pregnancies, sexually transmitted diseases, anxiety disorder, depression, attempting suicide, experiencing domestic or sexual violence, difficulties with academics, employment, or relationships, hallucinations, memory disturbances, or sleep disturbances.

Impact on Physical Health

The ACE study found that children who had experienced maltreatment were more likely to suffer from a variety of serious medical problems, including cancer, heart disease, lung disease, liver disease, autoimmune deficiencies, hypertension, diabetes, asthma, and obesity as adults.

Impact on Spiritual Health

Spiritual injuries from child sexual abuse or child maltreatment might include negative shifts in victims' perception of God (e.g., perceiving God as cruel, unfair, punitive, and distant), a ruptured relationship with God (e.g., feeling unloved by God), disruptions of faith (e.g., doubting God's existence), decreased involvement in organized religion (e.g., less willing to attend formal religious events), and a decline in spiritual well-being and functioning (e.g., feeling angry, guilty, or disconnected from one's sense of personal spirituality). Children who have suffered sexual abuse often endure spiritual injury and may feel guilty, doubtful of God's existence, or believe that God is unjust. Victims report a sense of enhanced betrayal when their abuser is a person they perceived as holy, and numerous studies have found that spiritual injuries are more pronounced in instances when the perpetrator is a member of the clergy.

CHAPTER FOUR

. . . .

PEOPLE WHO SEXUALLY ABUSE CHILDREN

Because of the heinous nature of child sexual abuse, it is easy to assume that those who perpetrate it must be easily identifiable as monsters or creeps with a trench coat, hiding in the shadows. But this image is inaccurate and harmful. In fact, there is no stereotype for people who sexually abuse children: They are male and female. They are young and old. They are often religious. They are often in positions of respect and authority within the community. Instead of focusing on personality or characteristics of offenders, churches can protect their children by focusing on identifiable behaviors they use to access, groom, and eventually abuse children. As one expert testified, "Their sexual behavior is often repetitive and highly predictable. Knowledge of these sexual-behavioral patterns is extremely valuable."[1] Understanding the behavior and methods used by those who sexually abuse children is paramount in implementing policies that protect them. When churches know how offenders operate, they can take proactive measures to identify their behavior and protect kids from child sexual abuse.

Two necessary components for any offender when sexually victimizing a child are access[2] and control.[3] The offender must have access to the child in order to perpetrate the abuse. Similarly, without some degree of control, the offender is unable to victimize children or ensure their silence. Three common methods used by people who sexually abuse in securing access to and control of children are: (1) authority, (2) trust, and (3) physical force,[4] or threats.[5]

OFFENDERS USE	TO GAIN	SO THEY
▶ Authority ▶ Trust ▶ Physical Force or Threats	▶ Access ▶ Control	▶ Sexually Abuse

Describing offenders by their relationship with the child, however, is a helpful way to talk about these three methods.[6] The three primary categories of offenders are the stranger, the acquaintance, and the intra-familial offender.[7] Churches may encounter all three categories, and so the Policy should address all three.

Stranger Offender

A stranger offender can be someone that the child has never seen, or someone with whom the child has only had minimal prior interactions,[8] and is by far the smallest category of people who sexually abuse children.[9] Stranger offenders secure access and control over children with authority, trust, and physical force/threats but most frequently utilize physical force/threats.

Physical Force and Threats

Due to the fact that there is no relationship between the offender and the child, the primary method a stranger molester uses to gain access and control of a child is physical force or threatened physical force.[10] It usually involves the physical force that is necessary to gain a victim's compliance, such as holding the child, physically removing the child to a specific location, or confining the child.[11]

Authority

The authority method is also utilized when the stranger has actual or perceived authority. Most children are raised to submit to those in authority—parents, teachers, religious leaders, and baby-sitters.[12] Stranger offenders possess a unique opportunity to access and control a child when they are an authoritative figure or deceive the child into believing that they have that authority.[13] For example, a uniformed police officer or perhaps a worship leader whom a child would recognize from the church's worship service but has no relationship with the child.

Trust

It is common knowledge that most children are taught not to trust strangers.[14] Thus, when people who sexually abuse children utilize trust to abuse a child they do not know, they convince the child that they are not strangers and can be trusted. The stronger offender must disarm the child of any preconceptions he or she may have about the meaning of the word "stranger."[15] This is usually accomplished without much difficulty due to the fact that children can be easily influenced by adults. Dr. David Warden, a psychologist at the University of Strathclyde in the United Kingdom, writes:

> No matter how intelligent the child, he or she does not see the world through skeptical adult eyes. . . . Children live very much in the present. They can't foresee someone's actions or judge their intentions, certainly not at primary school age. They have a very weak understanding of motives, they simply take someone at face value. The concept of stranger danger is difficult, because it clashes with the social constraints on children to be polite to adults. Research suggests that children don't really know what a stranger is. They feel that once someone tells his name, he ceases to be a stranger.[16]

The younger the child, the easier it is for stranger offenders to lure the child into believing that they are not strangers.[17] Once that belief has been set aside, the offender is a significant step closer to obtaining the necessary trust needed to sexually abuse.

Acquaintance Offender

An acquaintance offender is a non-family member—such as a family friend, clergy member, next-door neighbor, pediatrician, teacher, or church volunteer—who is acquainted with the child or the child's parents.[18] Acquaintance offenders will often work at positioning themselves "where they can meet children and have the opportunity to interact with children in an unsupervised way."[19] Kenneth Lanning helpfully explains that "[t]he acquaintance molester, by definition, is one of us. He is not simply an anonymous, external threat. He cannot be identified by physical description and, often, not even by 'bad' character traits. Without specialized training or experience and an objective perspective, he cannot easily be distinguished from others."[20]

The acquaintance offender is a larger category than the stranger offender. In fact, one study found that a "[A] child is three times more likely to be molested by a recognized, trusted adult than by a stranger."[21] Acquaintance offenders also utilize authority, trust, and physical force or threats to obtain access and control over children. Acquaintance offenders generally prefer to leverage trust to gain access and control.

Trust

The acquaintance molester attains access and control of the child by engaging in a process that is designed to secure the trust of the child and parent.[22] One scholar has described childhood trust as the "chosen battleground" for acquaintance molesters,[23] and this battle is commonly referred to as the "grooming process."[24] The acquaintance molester has the unique ability to identify with children. Kenneth Lanning describes how "[h]e knows how to talk to children, but more importantly, he knows how to listen to them."[25] A convicted pedophile details how "[t]here's a process of obtaining the child's friendship and, in my case, also obtaining the family's friendship and their trust. When you get their trust, that's when the child becomes vulnerable, and you can molest the child."[26] He continues,

> As far as the children goes [sic], they're kind of easy. You befriend them. You take them places. You buy them gifts. . . . Now in the process of grooming the child, you win his trust and I mean, the child has a look in his eyes—it's hard to explain—you just have to kind of know the look. You know when you've got that kid. You know when that kid trusts you.[27]

To secure this trust, the acquaintance offender grooms child victims by providing a variety of services and gifts, including but not limited to attention, affection, kindness, privileges, recognition, alcohol, drugs, money, and pornography.[28] Sometimes, the acquaintance offender will encourage his own children to befriend the target child in order to provide the opportunity to facilitate the grooming process.[29] The trust that develops as a result of the grooming process will often reduce the child's inhibitions and increase the offender's control over the child.[30] This toxic trust eventually renders the child virtually helpless, creating an environment for ongoing abuse, while increasing the likelihood that the victim will remain silent.[31] When asked how he kept his victims from reporting, a person who admitted to raping over one hundred victims reported,

> Well, first of all I've won all their trust. They think I'm the greatest living thing that ever lived. Their families think I'm the greatest thing that ever lived. Because I'm so nice

to them and I'm so kind and so—there's just nobody better
to that person than me. If it came down to, you know,
it came down to, "I have a little secret, this is our little
secret," then it would come down to that, but it didn't have
to usually come down to that. It's almost an unspoken
understanding.[32]

Not only do acquaintance offenders seek the trust of the child,
but often they first groom the child's guardian or guardians.[33] The
rationale behind this objective is that offenders will have greater
access to the child if they secure the guardian's trust first.[34]

The trust developed between an acquaintance offender and
the child and family is often made possible by the position of the
offender.[35] For example, children may develop a trusting relationship with next-door neighbors who have spent years fostering
a "friendship" with the children and their parents. On the other
hand, children may get into a vehicle alone with a youth pastor,
whom they barely know, simply because of the trust they or their
family may have for pastors. Often, acquaintance offenders will
exploit their position in order to open the door to a successful
grooming process.[36]

Authority

Though children may be taught to avoid the attention of strangers, they are generally instructed to "be obedient and affectionate
with any adult entrusted with their care."[37] As a result, acquaintance
offenders are often in a position to exploit their position of authority in order to access and silence children. This is most common
in positions of authority that have substantive exposure with children, such as family friends, teachers, camp counselors, baby-sitters,
clergy members, and any type of youth worker.[38] A classic example of
this dynamic is the abuse perpetrated upon a young Christa Brown
by her church youth pastor, Eddie. In her book, *This Little Light*,

Brown recounts how the acquaintance offender used his authority as a pastor to manipulate her into submission.[39] She writes:

> Eddie [pastor] always said that God had chosen me for something special. I guess I really wanted to believe that. Doesn't every kid want to think they're special? Besides, who was I to question a man of God? It wasn't my place. My role was to be submissive.[40]

Not only does authority provide the acquaintance offender with access to the child, but it often can be exploited to maintain the child's silence.[41] In general, direct requests for silence from those in authority have been proven to significantly impact compliance of both adults and children.[42] More specifically, children often delay or even fail to report sexual abuse "[b]ecause they are loathe to disobey an authority figure who has ordered silence."[43] In addition to simply instructing the child to remain silent, acquaintance offenders also employ threats, fear, blackmail, embarrassment, and confusion.[44]

Physical Force and Threats

There is no doubt that certain acquaintance offenders use physical force to exert sufficient control over the child in order to facilitate the abuse.[45] However, due to their ability to successfully manipulate issues of trust and authority, physical force is the least used method of acquaintance offenders to establish access and control over victims.[46] An acquaintance offender who uses physical force to control the child is more likely to be reported to law enforcement and identified by the child who has been victimized.[47] Use or the threat of physical force is most common with acquaintance offenders when the child resists the sexual demands of the offender or expresses intent to disclose the abuse.[48]

Intra-Familial Offender

An intra-familial offender is related to the victim and is someone who usually, but not always, lives in the same house as the victim such as a father, mother, sibling, or grandparent.[49] Some scholars consider a live-in boyfriend or girlfriend of the child's parent to be classified as an intra-familial.[50] The intra-familial offender is generally considered the largest of the three child molester categories, with one study finding that 68 percent of the admitted offenders sexually victimized a child within their family.[51] By the nature of the relationship, most intra-familial offenders have fairly trouble-free access to the target child.[52] Because of greater accessibility, intra-familial victims tend to be overall younger than non-familial victims.[53]

The primary challenge for the intra-familial offender is not access, but the ability to exert sufficient control in order to both abuse and silence the victim.[54] A seemingly greater correlation and interplay exists between the use of trust, authority, and physical force utilized by the intra-familial offender than with the other two categories.[55] However, for the sake of maintaining consistency, each method will be reviewed separately.

Authority

Authority is the primary manner in which many intra-familial offenders maintain long-term control over their victims.[56] This control derives from their parental-type authority, coupled with the fact that they are often the primary provider for the family's basic mental and physical necessities.[57] For example, the intra-familial offenders will often exercise authority over the child through exploiting the fact that they are the family provider, and that disclosing the sexual abuse will have devastating consequences upon the family.[58] This exploitation of authority to perpetrate abuse and silence is often augmented in some degree by the trust a child has in the abuser's role as a caretaker.[59] Furthermore, intra-familial offenders often exercise their authority with older children through the use of physical force and threats.[60]

The use of authority by intra-familial offenders is not limited to just caregivers. Any family member is capable of using or attempting to use authority as a mechanism to control the child for the purpose of facilitating abuse. However, when the abuser is not a caregiver, the effectiveness of this method will largely depend upon whether the child perceives the intra-familial abuser to have such authority.[61]

Trust

The trust a parent or family member has with a child often provides the necessary control to perpetuate long-term abuse.[62] Intra-familial offenders often subject the child victim to abuse through a distorted combination of authority and trust. When children are young, their knowledge of sexual matters is limited, and they often do not appreciate the wrongfulness of the offender's behavior.[63] However, as the child grows older and begins to comprehend the wrongfulness of the abuse, they fear negative consequences to others and also begin to feel responsible for their own abuse.[64] Consequently, intra-familial offenders manipulate and distort this familial position to secure acceptance and sexual intimacy with the child. This is tragically illustrated by the defendant who took his thirteen-year-old daughter on a camping trip and told her that "having sexual intercourse with him was the only way she could prove her love for him."[65]

Trust is also utilized by intra-familial offenders to keep child victims silent. The survival of children is largely dependent upon a successful attachment between them and their caregivers.[66] As a result, children often make every effort to block out the abuse in order to facilitate a "trusting" attachment to the abusive caregiver.[67] Not only will children unilaterally maintain silence as a mode of self-protection, but they will also remain silent if instructed to do so by the intra-familial offender.[68] A relationship based upon loyalty, devotion, and trust will foster "an overwhelming incentive for a child to abide by a parental request to conceal information."[69]

Physical Force and Threats

Intra-familial offenders often use some degree of physical force when the child is a family member.[70] The degree of physical force used by intra-familial offender is generally minimal with victims up to the age of eleven.[71] Often, this is "instrumental force" associated with the offender grabbing, carrying, or confining the child for the purpose of accomplishing the sexual act.[72] As children age, the amount of physical force used to perpetrate abuse often increases.[73] This increased force serves to prevent or discourage any resistance by the child.[74] Additionally, as with stranger and acquaintance offenders, intra-familial offenders often use threats to discourage the reporting of abuse (e.g., threatening to abuse a younger sibling instead if the child resists or tells).[75]

Policy Worksheet: People Who Sexually Abuse Children

Sample Policy Language:

People who sexually abuse children utilize authority, trust, or physical force/threats to gain access and control over children so they can perpetrate the abuse.

Would your church like to include a statement on each category of offender? _____ yes _____ no

If yes, consider this sample policy language:

The three primary categories of people who sexually abuse children are the stranger, the acquaintance, and the intra-familial offender.

Stranger offenders are people that the child has never seen, or people with whom the child has had only minimal prior interactions. Stranger offenders secure access and control over children with authority, trust, and physical force/threats but most frequently utilize physical force/threats and are the smallest category of offenders.

Acquaintance offenders are non-family members—such as a family friend, clergy member, next-door neighbor, pediatrician, teacher, or church volunteer—who is acquainted with the child or the child's parents. Acquaintance offenders generally prefer to leverage trust to gain access and control. To secure this trust, the acquaintance offender grooms child victims by providing a variety of services and gifts, including but not limited to attention, affection, kindness, privileges, recognition, alcohol, drugs, money, and pornography. The trust that develops as a result of the grooming process will often reduce the child's inhibitions and increase the offender's control over the child. This toxic trust eventually renders the child virtually helpless, creating an environment for ongoing abuse, while increasing the likelihood that the victim will remain silent.

Intra-familial offenders are related to the victim and are people who usually, but not always, live in the same house as the victim. The intra-familial offender is generally considered the largest of the three child molester categories. Because of greater accessibility, intra-familial victims tend to be overall younger than non-familial victims. The primary challenge for the intra-familial molester is not access, but the ability to exert sufficient control in order to both abuse and silence the victim. A seemingly greater correlation and interplay exists between the use of trust, authority, and physical force utilized by the intra-familial offender.

Policy Section Two

Protective Practices

Healthy adult-child relationships are critical to children's development.[1] And yet, if an adult in their lives is abusing them, the abuse is a terrible detriment to their growth. If children are being hurt in the very institution that is meant to nurture their spiritual development, it does not matter how excellent the church's programming is. Safety is a baseline of any church's ministry to children.

A well-formed Policy encourages healthy adult-child relationships by ensuring that the staff and volunteers who serve their children align with the community's values, by delineating between safe and unsafe behaviors, and by ensuring that the community's routines protect children. Protective practices help churches to put in place a foundation of safety and accountability that can then be built upon in wonderful ways to help children grow in their spiritual life. At their heart, protective practices promote safe, life-giving interactions while prohibiting risky and abusive interactions.

The following chapters explore best practices that can help protect children. Chapter Five outlines how to account for children's safety while your church hires staff and recruits volunteers. Chapter Six delineates between safe and risky behaviors. Chapter Seven discusses community routines and how to promote safety within these routines.

CHAPTER FIVE

. . . .

SCREENING

Every church wants to hire employees and recruit volunteers who will serve the congregation well. Staff and volunteers should fit the congregation's vision, culture, and values. Hiring and recruiting practices should be designed to select individuals who are best able to care for children and develop lasting mentorships. Whether the process is formalized or not, every church is encouraged to develop some process to ensure they hire well-qualified applicants and recruit volunteers who will support the youth and children's ministry. The following chapter outlines various ways a church can account for protecting its children during their hiring and recruiting process.

Adding measures to protect children into the hiring and recruiting process is a vital component of any Policy. It is not unusual for high-risk offenders to look for careers that provide the most opportunities to access and abuse children. Becoming a church employee or volunteer provides significant access to children. Any church with children in attendance will attract people who want to sexually abuse children. As sex offender treatment expert Dr. Anna Salter writes, "Any situation that provides ideal conditions for pedophiles will draw them, and it will be very difficult to distinguish them from their nonpedophilic and entirely normal colleagues. Look at any arrangement where pedophiles will thrive, and you will find pedophiles."[1]

Churches can take action to offset this risk by screening staff and volunteers who work with children. In one church, a search committee almost hired a youth worker with an extensive history of employment in Christian organizations. He had a great résumé and close connections to other churches. The applicant's background check did not list any offenses, and he looked like a great hire. After speaking with several references, however, the church's leadership discovered that the applicant once had an abusive relationship with a child he met at his previous employment, but he was never convicted. Assessing the applicant from multiple angles revealed more, critical information. Calling references during the hiring process potentially saved children in their church from harm.

Churches must assess employees and volunteers before allowing them access to children. Thorough screenings may catch the most obvious or egregious offenders. Screening practices can also function as a deterrent, alerting would-be offenders of the church's vigilance and commitment to child safety. In many instances, an applicant seeking to abuse a child will look for an organization that provides easy access to children; churches with thorough screening procedures communicate that they are not such a place.

A thorough screening may not necessarily identify someone as a child abuser, as that is a difficult task, but it can help the church determine if the applicant is an appropriate fit for the position. Screening yields valuable information about potential employees and volunteers that enables churches to gauge whether they may uphold the church's values, will work well with other employees and volunteers, follow the Policy, report suspected abuse, and remain alert to potential threats against children.

Churches must include screening procedures in their Policy and identify who will be required to go through which measures. This chapter outlines some of the best practices in a screening process to assess applicants and volunteers who will have access to children.[2] These best practices are tools that a church can use to help shape the process of bringing on new staff and volunteers or that a church can add to their already-defined process. Furthermore, these screening tools can be applied in different ways. Churches will have to decide which positions need which screening tools.

Screening Tools

The tools for screening applicants include written applications, background checks, social media reviews, reference checks, and interviews. These screening tools allow churches to examine applicants from several different perspectives, giving them invaluable information about those who may have access to children. The screening tools also give churches permission to follow their intuition. As Gavin de Becker explains, "Intuition is always right in at least two important ways: 1) It is always in response to something. 2) It always has your best interest at heart."[3] Churches can take the information they learn about applicants in the screening process and develop an informed opinion about them. Churches must allow themselves time to listen to their intuition. When evaluating applicants, churches can slow down the process, think about their reactions, follow up with the applicants, and examine which applicant is right for the position and for the church.

Written Applications

The written application can be the first step of your screening process. Requiring that applicants fill out a written application:

- Saves time by weeding out applicants who are obviously a poor fit for your church or for the position.
- Formalizes the application process and thus communicates that this is a serious position.

- Puts the applicant on notice immediately that your church is serious about child protection and expects full compliance with the Policy. Have a place on the application where applicants acknowledge they have read and understand the Policy.
- Allows the church to easily verify the information provided by the applicant.
- Documents applicants' answers in their own words, thus creating a record that may be referenced throughout the screening process and, if necessary, once employment has begun.

Use the application as a place to gather technical information on a potential employee or volunteer. Such information may include contact information, educational history, employment/volunteer history, and references. Additionally, ask applicants to disclose criminal history and violent or abusive behavior. Though the application is dependent on self-report and the applicant may fail to disclose, just the process of asking for this disclosure may serve as a potential deterrent. At the very least, it puts the applicant on notice from the start that your church takes child protection seriously.

If your church prefers that the application serve the additional purpose of getting to know the applicant, you may wish to ask some open-ended questions about the applicant's experience working with youth, personal testimony, views on theological issues, and approach to child protection. The answers provided by the applicant can then serve as additional material for the church to verify or clarify with references or during the interview. Appendix Two provides sample written applications for adults and for teens.

Your application should also include a consent authorization. Properly protecting children today means that you will need to ask applicants for a considerable amount of personal information, and this can understandably make some applicants uncomfortable. It is always best to learn of an applicant's discomfort with your screening process before either of you have invested time in getting to know each other. Applicants who know what to expect can decide in advance if they feel comfortable participating in your screening process and have the opportunity to decline to participate if they are not comfortable with you conducting a background check or contacting references. Include an indemnification clause releasing the references from any potential liability that may result from speaking to the church, and the church from any potential liability that may result from conducting the screening or acting on the information received. The clause can also include a statement that the church will keep a person's application file confidential, except in instances when they discover child abuse. [4]

Because employment law can be complicated and differs from state to state, and even city to city, check with an employment attorney or contact your state's fair employment agency to determine what information you may ask about and use in making employment decisions, and to ensure that the language you develop for the screening and hiring section of your Policy and application do not violate any laws.

Background Checks

Background checks are a basic minimum precaution. Background checks may protect a church from convicted offenders, and like all screening measures, they may deter some offenders by indicating that the church is serious about child protection. It is common knowledge that public schools require all prospective teachers to undergo mandatory, criminal background checks. Yet each year, individuals who have been convicted of criminal offenses still submit applications with the Department of Education and attempt to gain access to vulnerable children.[5] While there is no comparable data to analyze for private youth-serving organizations, the draw for sex offenders in churches is the same as that in public schools: easy access to children. As such, a church that neglects to conduct background checks may unintentionally hire a known offender, and in so doing place its children in danger and itself at risk for a negligent-hiring lawsuit. In fact, it is because of this risk that liability insurers are increasingly requiring background checks and other screening procedures as a prerequisite for coverage.[6] Background checks should also be conducted on all staff and volunteers.

To find a reputable screening company, you might ask other youth-serving organizations for recommendations or check out the National Association of Professional Background Screeners' (NAPBS) website, which provides a directory of regional and national member companies, as well as guidance for what to look for in choosing a screening company. At the minimum, make sure the company you choose follows all industry standards, provides you with the notices and consent forms you will need to provide your applicants, and has a thorough understanding of the laws relevant to screening in your state.

Because different background check provides research different information, you will want to ask all vendors you consider using what packages and information they provide. Do they only conduct statewide checks, or do they cover federal databases as well? Do they only report on felonies, or misdemeanors too? Do they only report convictions, or charges and arrests too?[7] What records does the company have access to and how often do they update their data? In general, the information you receive will depend on the information you ask for, and the more information you want the more it will cost. If possible, it is best for churches to obtain background checks that provide the most data. Understanding that resources may limit some churches in obtaining the most comprehensive background check available, it is critical that at the very least the background check provide a local, state, and federal criminal records check. Options from commercial companies may include any of the following:

- Confirmation of education
- Local criminal record check
- State criminal record check
- FBI criminal record check
- State central child/dependent adult abuse registry check
- State sex offender registry check
- Motor vehicle record check
- Professional disciplinary board background check

Be aware that criminal background checks do not inform you about all court-involvement an applicant may have had. Because criminal background checks only check for criminal convictions, these reports do not include information on family or civil court cases (including cases about child abuse), they do not include an application's arrest history or other legal complaints. In addition, state criminal background checks do not include criminal cases that were brought in other states or at the federal level. Even reports about criminal convictions occurring in the state you are searching may exclude certain crimes, such as non-violent offenses, misdemeanors, historical crimes, cases where the record was expunged or sealed, and cases that should have been included but were excluded due to clerical error. Before relying on a report from a criminal background check, make sure you understand what information you are being provided, and what you are not being provided.

When a background check yields any result, consult with your GRACE Certification Specialist or another trained expert who can interpret the data. Even non-sexual, non-violent offenses can be red flags and cause for concern as it relates to the care and protection of children. For example, an offense with alcohol, such as DUI, needs to be explored because alcohol can be used to groom a child for abuse or simply because the applicant may be entrusted to transport children. Furthermore, in some degree any conviction shows an individual's willingness to break rules and boundaries and should be discussed directly with the individual.

Social Media Searches

While background checks must be a central component of a church's screening process, even these only report applicants' criminal history if they have been convicted of a crime. Because most instances of child sexual abuse are unreported or not prosecuted, offenders can easily move from organization to organization without having a conviction show up on their official record.[8] Jerry Sandusky would have passed a criminal background check for most of his life because he had no criminal convictions. Many other people who harm children have likewise never been convicted, but signs of their harmful behavior may surface in other areas.

Internet and social media searches provide valuable information not found in applicants' official records. Your church should conduct Internet searches for all of an applicant's known names, email addresses, and screen names. You should also check information available on applicants' social media accounts. Some of the main platforms to search include Instagram, Facebook, Twitter, and Pinterest, though new social media sites and apps are constantly changing, so be sure to check with someone who has current knowledge of popular sites for a particular applicant's age group.

If Internet or social media searches reveal concerning information, such as sexually explicit photos or videos or sexual language, this applicant is not a good fit for your church. If the applicant has a "friend list" comprised primarily of children, or in the case of a child applicant primarily of children who are significantly younger than the applicant, do not offer the position to this applicant. Be similarly concerned if an applicant is liking, commenting on, or sharing numerous photos of unrelated children, or if an applicant's comments are themselves indicative of grooming or other concerning behaviors. Be aware, too, that a social media search may reveal information that does not jeopardize children's safety but shows that an applicant is not a good fit for the position.

During their social media checks, churches have found:

- An adult applicant who "liked" thousands of pictures of children, including hundreds of pictures where children were in states of undress or making seductive faces at the camera
- A forty-eight-year-old applicant who posted on a seventeen-year-old's picture "Wow—beautiful is all I can say. Marry me please???"
- An applicant who shared photos of her neighbor's children, her nieces and nephews, and children from around the neighborhood, accompanied by possessive commentary (e.g., "my sweeties"), pet names, and stories of all the overnight trips she took them on.
- An Internet search of an applicant's screen name hit immediately to a video—that the applicant himself had posted—of the applicant engaging in sexual behavior, as well as other lewd postings. These worrisome posts were interspersed among the applicant's professional postings in online educational forums.
- An applicant posted statements and information that demonstrated she was not an appropriate fit to serve the children in the church.

Reference Checks

While background checks and social media searches are important, they are not sufficient. Reference checks determine if previous employers or personal contacts have concerns about potential staff and volunteers. In over fifteen years of working with youth, many former employees have asked one youth pastor to serve as a reference, yet potential employers have only contacted him one time. While reference checks may be the most helpful screening tool, they also may be the most neglected. Reference checks protect children because the references give the church valuable, outside perspective on the applicant. Gavin de Becker, a national expert on violence prediction, calls employers' "failure to take the obvious step of calling references . . . an epidemic in America."[9]

The Policy should stipulate that the church contacts at least two professional references for all applicants for a staff or volunteer position, even if they are minors. While applicants often supply a list of references, any references the candidate supplies will be of limited value. A church should contact all applicants' previous employers, even if they do not specify the employer as a reference.

The Policy may also stipulate that the church directly ask the reference for other people with whom the applicant worked. Collateral references—people the applicant did not directly supply—are, in general, more valuable sources of information. The church should seek out and speak with these references as well. References whom the applicant would not expect the church to call may be more willing to speak freely about the applicant and give honest feedback.

The church may also wish to ask applicants for personal references. This may be necessary in cases when an applicant does not have previous employment, such as a teenage applicant. Personal references should be individuals who have supervised the applicant's interactions with children (e.g., the parent of a child the applicant has babysat) and can attest to the applicant's character (e.g., a teacher who knows the applicant well).

Even if the reference submitted a letter of recommendation, the church should also speak with each reference. Begin by asking references to verify factual information about an applicant's résumé and application, including educational background, time of employment, and job duties. It is reasonable for you to expect that the information you receive from references match the information submitted by the applicant. Follow up on inconsistencies, understanding that direct falsehoods on a résumé or employment application are not a good sign. Though a minor inconsistency may be nothing more than a careless error and even outright falsehoods may have a reasonable explanation, at the very least such instances should be flagged for further clarification.

On a more substantive level, the church should ask open-ended questions about the applicant's behavior around children (see box for sample questions). At some point, churches must directly ask references to share any and all concerns they may have about the applicant.[10] As references answer these questions, listen for hesitancy, ambiguousness, or evasiveness in their tone or answers, and if noted, request elaboration. Research indicates that references may be reluctant to share negative opinions about applicants, especially as related to concerns regarding child abuse.[11] As such, it is critical that you read between the lines when speaking to references, ask follow-up questions, and pay attention to indirect and unspoken feedback.

Sample Questions for References[12]

- Can you describe the applicant's character and personality?
- In what capacities have you observed the applicant interact with children?
- How would you describe the applicant's interactions with children?
- What strengths does the applicant have in relating to children?
- What challenges does the applicant have in relating to children?
- Would you have any hesitations allowing _____ to supervise and care for children (or youth)?
- Have you seen the applicant discipline youth?
- Would you want this individual working in your organization again in the future?

If, during the course of a conversation, a reference reveals that an applicant previously jeopardized the safety of children, violated a child protection policy, did not report suspicions of abuse, or was alleged to have personally harmed a child, this applicant is not safe to hire. If an applicant was asked to leave or not rehired at a former place of employment due to concerns regarding child safety, do not hire the applicant. If the previous institution believed they had enough information that warranted keeping the applicant away from the children in their own institution, take that information seriously, even if the reference cannot or will not elaborate further.

When possible, churches should conduct reference checks before interviews, but at the very least, they should complete reference checks before they officially hire applicants. By speaking to references before the interview, churches can question applicants about any concerns that arise or cancel interviews completely if reference checks yield "deal-breaking" information.

Suggestions for Conducting Reference Checks

- Ask prospective hires for at least two references that have previously supervised their youth work.
- Call the references before the interview.
- When speaking to a reference, ask open-ended questions and avoid leading questions.
- Listen for hesitation and pauses, and ask for elaboration.
- Request that in addition to extolling the virtues of the applicant, the reference communicate any concerns, no matter how trivial.
- Ask references if they would hire the applicant again.
- Ask the references for one or two other people who know the candidate and could be contacted.

Interviews

Interviews provide churches with the opportunity to assess whether applicants are well suited for the position, including but not limited to their ability to keep children safe and abide by the Policy. Churches can hold interviews for all individuals, including adolescents, who are applying to work with children or youth.

Depending upon the applicant, the interviews can be more or less extensive and more or less formal.

A thorough interview will allow applicants to educate the church about themselves and allow the church to educate applicants about the Policy. During the dialogue, remain alert to any indicators that applicants may not keep children safe. Interviews allow churches to develop gut-instincts about whether they can trust an applicant to work well with children, and churches should follow these gut-instincts.

Assessing Applicants

When interviewing applicants, you can gain valuable information by asking the right questions and listening both to what the applicants say and do not say. Make sure to review an applicant's résumé and written application before the interview, highlighting any inconsistencies, noticeable gaps, or concerns. Have these documents on hand when conducting the interview, so that you can clarify ambiguities (e.g., does a gap of two years mean the applicant is omitting a place of employment where things did not go well?), note inconsistencies (an applicant who lies on the application may do so in seemingly minor ways—job title or dates of employment—and later forget the specifics of the lies), and voice concerns ("You state that you have a Master of Divinity from this seminary, but only list one year there. All of their ordination tracks are four years"; or " You indicate that you were fired from your previous job, can you tell us what happened?"). There are certain uncomfortable questions you may need to ask (such as "Have you ever consumed alcohol or drugs while working with children?" or "Have you ever harmed a child?"), and it is best to do so directly, rather than wondering or trying to guess what an applicant's answer would be.[13] The following box gives sample questions that churches can use during an interview. The list is not exhaustive, nor should churches use every question. Your church will need to decide which questions they want to prioritize, as not all questions will fit every context.

Sample Interview Questions[14]

- Please tell us about your experience working with children.
- For younger applicants with less experience:
    Do you have younger siblings?
    If so, do you help take care of them?
    If not, have you helped care for other children, such as cousins, or neighbors?
- Why do you want this job? Why are you interested in working with children? [Be wary of answers that focus on children filling the adult's needs (e.g., "children are non-judgmental and make me feel good about myself") rather than the adult meeting the child's needs ("I'm good at helping children learn to study the Bible")] What do you find most rewarding/challenging about working with children?
- Describe a child you enjoyed working with and a child that was particularly challenging.
- What strategies do you use to respond to challenging behaviors?
- Have you ever encountered problems with children you were caring for?
- Have you ever been in an emergency situation while taking care of a child?
- What is your opinion on drugs/alcohol use for adults/teenagers? Do you use drugs/alcohol? If so, when? Have you ever used drugs or alcohol before or while you were caring for children?
- In a situation where you may have lost your temper with children:
    – What was the trigger?
    – How did you manage it?
    – What was the outcome?
    – What strategies did you implement upon reflection?
- Have you ever mistreated a child? Have you ever abused a child?
- Are there any children with whom you would not wish to work and, if so, why?

Sample Interview Questions (continued)

- Is there a specific age/sex you prefer to work with? How would you feel about working with a different age/sex? [Some child abusers select victims with specific characteristics, so be wary of inflexibility. At the same time applicants may request a specific age group/sex because of previous experience. Ask some follow-up questions to determine if there is cause for concern.]
- Have you ever suspected that one of the children in your care was being abused? [Denial would be concerning.] What type of supervisory situation do you prefer? [If your Policy requires close supervision, an independent applicant who resists supervision may not be the right fit. Child abusers seek settings with minimal supervision, so be wary if an applicant stresses the importance of privacy and complete autonomy in interacting with youth.]
- What would your friends, colleagues, or supervisors say about how you interact with youth? Is there anyone who might suggest that you should not work with youth? Why or why not?
- Please outline any action taken against you in relation to working or volunteering with children. This may include, but is not limited to, allegations and disciplinary action.
- Do you own a gun? Where do you use it? Is there ever a time when you might think it would be appropriate to bring a gun or weapon to the church?
- What other hobbies or activities do you enjoy? [Determine if applicants have mature, adult relationships and interests that do not involve youth. If an applicant reports relationships with youth to the exclusion of adults—be wary.]
- If you were me conducting this interview, is there something you would make sure to ask? Is there something I should have asked about? Is there anything else you would like to tell us?
- Do you have any questions for us?

While it is important to be thorough, remember that there are limits to what can be asked in an interview. Avoid discriminating, harassing, or invasive lines of questioning. In particular, never ask applicants if they were sexually abused or maltreated as a child.

This question could be very triggering for a survivor, and there is no evidence that just because a person has been abused as a child, they will abuse as an adult. Only a small number of victims have been identified as perpetrators.

These interviews should be conducted in person and before the applicant begins work. If churches get a concerning feeling at any point during the interview, they would be wise to trust their instinct and treat all misgivings seriously. Determining whether an applicant is a risk is nearly impossible given the constraints of the interview (e.g., no formal testing), that most individuals who abuse children are adept at lying,[15] and the improbability that an interviewer will be able to detect deceit or an unsavory character.[16] Interviewers can instead focus on what they are capable of: remaining alert to any indicators that applicants may not keep children safe and determining if the applicant is a good fit for the position. If anything about an applicant makes the church think they cannot keep children safe, they would be wise to deny that applicant.

Introducing the Policy

Along with getting to know applicants, the interview is a time for them to get to know the church. Interviews are a great opportunity to introduce the applicant to the Policy. The Centers for Disease Control (CDC) recommend that, before granting an interview, churches send applicants a copy of the Policy, require them to sign, acknowledging they received it, and inform them that the interviewer will discuss the Policy with them.[17]

During the interview, churches should summarize the main safety rules in the Policy and ask applicants how they would respond to hypothetical cases of Policy violations or child sexual abuse. As part of their discussion of the Policy, interviewers should also inform applicants that staff and children in the church are trained to identify and report Policy violations, grooming behaviors, and sexual abuse. Relaying this information lets potential offenders know that this church proactively protects its children. Such a message may deflect those sex offenders who are worried about getting caught or seeking easy opportunities to abuse.

Applicants committed to protecting children will welcome a discussion of child safety. In contrast, applicants who deflect a dialogue about the Policy may not abuse children themselves, but certainly may be less vigilant to keep children safe. It is important to take note of applicants' willingness to respond to hypothetical situations and their attitude toward the Policy.

Interviewers should also note any reservations in following the Policy or reporting abuse that the applicant may express. A single answer need not necessarily determine whether an applicant is selected or rejected, but it may provide valuable information about applicants' views on child protection. For instance, if they express hesitation about reporting in the context of a hypothetical case of child abuse, churches can fairly assume that these applicants will experience even greater hesitation when confronted with an actual case of child abuse.

Discussing the Policy upfront also ensures that applicants cannot later claim ignorance as an excuse for violating the Policy. In fact, one teacher who was convicted of sexually assaulting his students said that his school had a Policy, but they never discussed it. Instead, school leaders presumed that teachers had admirable intentions. He explained that he took advantage of this culture of secrecy to perpetrate his abuse and suggested that school officials might have deterred him from ever operating in their school had they been direct and strict about the Policy from the onset.

Conducting an Interview

- Always interview the potential employees in person, before putting them to work with children.
- When possible, have two different interviewers meet with the applicant and compare notes afterward.
  - Applicants who are looking to deceive the interviewer may craft their answers based on their perception of what the interviewer is looking to hear.
- Ask applicants to read through the Policy before the interview and ask them what their thoughts are.
  - Expressing displeasure about the Policy does not mean that applicants are abusers, but it probably means that they will be less vigilant about protecting children.
- Give applicants a hypothetical case of child abuse and ask how they would handle the situation.
  - If applicants express reservation about following church Policy for a hypothetical case, it is a fair assumption that they will hesitate when confronted with an actual case.
- Before making a job offer, take the time to observe the applicant working with children.
  - If you get a funny feeling watching the applicant's interactions with youth, respect that feeling.

Sample Hypothetical Cases

Gauge the applicant's response to scenarios involving boundary issues, youth protection polices, or adult-child interactions. Below are examples of some scenarios. Ask the applicant, "How would you respond to the following scenarios?"

- A five-year-old is crying and wants to go back to her caregivers.
- A toddler needs his diaper changed. When you take off his pants he says, "Are you going to hurt me?"
- Your male supervisor makes a remark about a twelve-year-old girl that borders on sexually inappropriate.
- Your fellow youth leader thinks the Policy is too extreme. She frequently spends time alone with various children in her group, so that she can develop a "close" relationship with them.

Adapted from the Centers for Disease Control and Prevention (2007).

Who Should Be Screened?

In developing a Policy on screening, churches should carefully consider anyone who might interact with the church's youth and children, especially those appointed to official positions (e.g., employees and volunteers). These individuals have access to children at the church, form relationships with families that extend beyond the church, and hold positions of trust. Before introducing an individual to children or teens, your church must do its due diligence, no matter how impressive the applicant or how urgent the need is for assistance. Your church should also consider church leaders and employees who do not interact directly children but hold positions of authority within the community. Consider which screening tools to use with which positions, including but not limited to:

1. Church employees
2. Volunteers
3. Church members
4. General employees, contractors, and subcontractors

It may be impossible to conduct full screenings for all of these categories. On the one hand, a full screening (using every screening tool) yields valuable information about a potential staff member or volunteer; yet, all churches may not be able to conduct such extensive research on every category of employee and volunteer. On the other hand, not screening at all leaves children and churches vulnerable. Thankfully, screenings are not all or nothing. Churches will need to determine which screening procedures to use for each category of staff or volunteer. Furthermore, churches can tailor each tool to each position. For example, a church may have a more extensive written application for staff members than for volunteers. Your church can work within its context to protect your children and making screening staff and volunteers an achievable process.

Church Employees

Churches must screen all employees. Such positions might include pastors, youth leaders, tutors, worship directors, counselors, mentors, nursery workers, security guards, and more depending on the community. When hiring for official positions, use as many screening tools as possible because any church employee will have a position of authority within the congregation.

Volunteers

Churches must also devise screening protocols for all volunteers within youth and children's ministries. In recent years, it has become increasingly common for youth-serving organizations to require anyone who might have contact with any child to undergo complete screenings. In other youth-serving organizations, this issue is handled by requiring only long-term youth volunteers to undergo complete screenings, while allowing ad-hoc volunteers (e.g., someone who supplies snacks for the youth group but does not participate) more limited screenings (e.g., instead of a formal interview, talk informally with the individual: How did you hear about this program? What is your connection to our church? Why do you want to volunteer?). On their own, these informal interviews are insufficient to protect the church's children, but they do hold some value in that they might at least serve to weed out the most obvious suspects.

Church Members

Whether they serve directly with children or not, churches should strongly consider screening anyone in a leadership or visible position within the church, including elders, deacons, board members, worship leaders, and anyone with keys to the church building. Some churches screen their members whether they directly serve with children or not. This may be a part of a church's process of joining a church, especially if the member expresses interest in volunteering.

Independent Contractors

Churches may also sponsor activities that are related to youth but are not directly under the youth department's auspices, such as Boy Scout or Girl Scout troops. In these situations, churches may reasonably expect the parent organization to screen their own staff, but the church must expressly inquire whether and how this screening has been done. A church should never assume that another organization has screened its youth workers.

In addition, churches should also screen people who are regularly on the premises when youth are present. Consider protocols for individuals who have only occasional access to children, such as caterers, contractors, and subcontractors (e.g., electricians). For these individuals, churches will need to determine whether the church has the resources to screen them or if the company providing the employees can assume that responsibility.

Policy Worksheet: Screening

Think about a hiring objective for your church:

[Faith Church] aims to hire employees and recruit volunteers to work with children who fit our

» Personality
» Vision
» Culture
» Theology
» Values
»
»
»

In keeping with our values of protecting the children in our care, as we hire employees or recruit volunteers, [Faith Church] will require

_____ Written Applications

_____ Background Checks

_____ Internet/Social Media Searches

_____ Reference Checks

_____ Interviews

Who Will Your Church Screen?

List your church employees (or categories of church employees):

List volunteers (or categories of volunteers, e.g., nursery help, youth group mentor, etc.):

List church leaders (or categories of church leaders, e.g., elders, deacons, etc.):

What screening procedures will you require of these?

Employee/ Volunteer	Written applications?	Background checks?	Internet Searches?	Reference Checks?	Interviews?

Sample Policy Language:

[Faith Church] requires the following screening procedures:

» The completion of a written application.
» At least two references to be contacted. These references should include (check all that your church will require):

- Previous employers
- At least one reference not supplied directly by the applicant
- Personal references if the applicant is under eighteen

» A background check that includes the following information (check all that your church will require):

- Confirmation of education
- Local criminal record check
- State criminal record check
- FBI criminal record check
- State central child/dependent adult abuse registry check
- State sex offender registry check
- Motor vehicle record check
- Professional disciplinary board background check

» An interview that explores a candidate's written application and introduces the child protection policy to the candidate.

If the screening process yields information that an individual abused a child in any way or has been convicted of a violent and/or sexual crime, that individual may not work with children in any capacity, and [Faith Church] will contact its GRACE Certification Specialist (or a similar child protection expert) about how to proceed. If the screening process shows that a candidate has ever been accused of a violent and/or sexual crime OR convicted of any other type of crime, [Faith Church] will consult with its GRACE Certification Specialist (or a similar child protection expert) to assess the situation.

CHAPTER SIX

. . . .

SAFE BEHAVIORS

Everyday, people who work with children face hard choices about appropriate and inappropriate behavior. Is it okay to hug a child? Is acceptable to give a child a ride home from youth group? What if a child has to use the bathroom? In childcare institutions, workers were surveyed about situations that arose where they required guidance on how to respond well. The scenarios they listed included,

- If a child has an accident
- If a child is bleeding on her leg and her tights need to be removed
- If a child comes up to give a hug
- If a child is crying and needs to be calmed down
- If a child throws up and needs help changing
- If a child spills food on his shirt and needs help changing
- If a child has a splinter and needs to be held so it can be removed

Anyone serving in youth or children's ministries, either as staff or as a volunteer, will face these or even more difficult choices about their behavior toward children. When churches proactively clarify safe behavior, they protect children and help adults. Before adult staff and volunteers are in a situation, wondering what to do, the Policy can guide them on how to interact with a child in a safe way.

The Policy can directly prohibit abusive or risky behaviors. Risky behavior helps conceal abuse. By promoting safe behavior, the Policy can cut down on situations where children are vulnerable—where a predator would have opportunity to harm them.

When communities practice safe behavior, they will more easily see the red flags of abusive behavior and be better prepared to respond to these red flags well. For example, in one community, a youth director was well known for spending special, alone time with particular children. He would invite a boy to play basketball at a gym where they would change into workout clothes in the locker room. The children at the church coveted these invitations, and the pastor used these times as a part of his mentoring program. Even if this pastor did so with the most pure motives, he did not model safe behavior. His actions normalized potentially abusive behavior— being alone with a child in an isolated, vulnerable setting. Maybe this pastor did not abuse children, but maybe someone else, with the same behavior patterns, did. The community would never know the difference because the pastor normalized the risky behavior and thus potentially helped conceal abuse. In contrast, when communities normalize safe behavior, actions that are abusive become easier to see. A Policy that clarifies how the community wants adults to interact with children helps adults and children. A thorough Policy will set interactive guidelines addressing adult-child ratios, extra attention, touch, sexual language, and media.

Adult-Child Ratios

Policies that require the presence of at least two adults in adult-child interactions are considered the gold standard of child protection and should be adopted whenever possible. While offenders can still act out, having two adults present makes offending harder, requiring more effort and thought than when one adult is present. In developing a Policy, your church should ask the staff to identify situations in which adults or older youth are typically alone with a child. Then, think about ways to ensure that two adults are present at those situations.

When considering which adults to supervise a children's room, choose adults who are not related or close friends. When close friends or family supervise children together, they typically have a harder time holding each other accountable. If a husband and wife or two brothers want to teach a children's class together, they must have a non-relative also present in the room to ensure safe adult-child ratios.

Other difficult but necessary situations that require adequate adult supervision are youth trips or events off church property. These situations pose challenges because they are events where children will be away from primary caregivers and engaging in vulnerable activities: changing, bathing, swimming, and sleeping. The Policy should stipulate that youth trips secure accommodations where children have private and separate quarters from the adult supervisors for changing, bathing, and sleeping.

Adults should have separate sleeping quarters, but they should still be able to supervise the youths' rooms to ensure children are well cared for and are following safety rules. While the practice of segregating youth helps to decrease their risk of abuse by adults, it also increases the opportunity for abuse by other youth. Roughly one-third of all sexual assaults against children are perpetrated by other youth,[1] and removing adults could potentially embolden youth who might otherwise be too inhibited to act on their abusive impulses. Maintaining some form of constant adult-supervision by two adults is necessary.

Potential Staff-Child Interactions

- Overnight youth department events and trips
- Youth staff or pastors offering to babysit
- Tutoring or music lessons
- Transporting children to or from youth events
- Taking a child on a special trip or out for a treat (e.g., pizza or ice cream)
- Youth staff or pastors hosting a Friday night lock-in, Sunday lunch, or Wednesday night Bible study

If this gold standard cannot be implemented, the Policy should advise on which activities staff and volunteers should avoid altogether and which activities they can creatively overcome adult-child isolation. Most churches rightfully consider certain one-on-one adult-child interactions as important elements of a child's personal and Christian discipleship. Churches should clearly articulate guidelines for decreasing the risk inherent in one-on-one adult-child interactions by insisting that interactions with one adult are observable and interruptible. Similarly, any off-site events at a home or private setting should still comply with the Policy by having two adults present or by being both observable and interruptible.

Observable Interactions

Church staff or volunteers who meet children for one-on-one mentoring or off-site events must manage the risk to the child by creatively making the interaction observable. For instance, a low-risk off-site event would have six youth leaders attending a Friday night youth group at the pastor's home because there would be high visibility with multiple adults and children present. Even in this scenario, leaders should remain in visible parts of the house, never alone with a child in a bedroom, for example. In contrast, a high-risk situation would be a youth director driving a child—alone—to a remote state park for a hike because there is low visibility and one adult. This type of event would not comply with Policy and should be prohibited.

Churches are encouraged to create a list of possible situations in which church professionals might interact with children off campus, and specify in their Policy which situations are considered high-risk and therefore prohibited and which are considered low risk and permitted. Churches should take the time to detail mitigating and aggravating risk factors surrounding these interactions, as well as tips on how to manage risk, so that church professionals have guidance when encountering situations not expressly listed in the Policy.

Interruptible Interactions

Even in observable, lower-risk interactions, if an adult must be alone with a child or multiple children, supervisors or caregivers should interrupt these interactions by dropping in unexpectedly. When adults meet with children of any age, they can extend open invitations to caregivers, informing them of the meeting and asking them to interrupt the youth programs or meetings whenever they want. When a Sunday school teacher is sick and has to miss class, the co-teacher can keep the classroom door open and invite the children's ministry director to stop by class. These invitations function as more than just a considerate accommodation. Good communication with caregivers and supervisors sets the tone for a safe, transparent youth department and reassures caregivers that the church is serious about eliminating opportunities for child sexual abuse.

If it is not possible to have two leaders in a room for regular group activities, such as Sunday school, other precautions can be taken to prevent abuse. Consider requiring that adults never be alone with one child at any given time and that if one adult is with two or more children, the adult should prop open the room's door.

Having a supervisor rotate in and out of the various youth groups can increase supervision and make the interactions observable and interruptible. However, it is important to note that the presence of multiple children is not necessarily a safeguard against sexual abuse. In fact, one study found that 55 percent of offenders had sexually abused when another child was present.[2] Accordingly, the use of the multiple-children-with-one-adult rule should only be used in readily observable and interruptible situations. Sunday school fits these qualifications because they occur at a time when the youth director, congregants, parents, and clergy are available to interrupt and observe a classroom as necessary. Youth programs (e.g., dance, art, or karate classes) led by one adult on weekday evenings, or at other times when the church is deserted, pose greater risks and churches should avoid relying on the presence of multiple children to safeguard against sexual abuse in these situations. See the box below for examples of other instances when a child might be alone with an adult or older youth during church programs or services.

Potential One-on-One Adult-Child Interactions	Safety Suggestions
Mentoring sessions	Set a time or place when a parent or supervisors will be present
Weekday youth group	Ask another employee or volunteer to assist
Youth group leader needs to leave group room	Have a "floating leader" available to transfer in
Taking children to the bathroom	See box below for precautionary measures
Transportation to youth events	Opt for group travel when possible
Children hanging out in the church after services or programs have ended when only a few stragglers remain	Make sure that spaces are locked as they empty out and that multiple adults are supervising the youth
Youth programs occurring when the church is empty	Ask other staff /volunteers to attend, or reschedule

Especially for younger children, maintaining interactions that are observable and interruptible becomes difficult when church staff and volunteers need to take a child to the bathroom. Churches should take time to discuss its diapering and toileting Policy, deciding on procedures that allow little ones to receive the toileting help they need with the safety they also need. Similar measures would apply to when a child needs help with a clothing change.

Suggestions to Consider for Toileting and Diapering

When a child uses a restroom, staff ensures:

- If a bathroom is not attached to the supervised program room, bring children to the bathroom in groups.
- Ensure the restroom is not occupied by an unknown individual before allowing children to use the facilities.
- Children are with an adult staff member and proceed in groups of three or more (e.g., one staff and two children or two staff and one child) when using the bathroom.
- Line-of-sound instead of line-of-sight supervision is maintained while children are using the facilities (i.e., the supervisor should be able to hear the child but not see them).
- If staff are assisting younger children, doors to the facility must remain open.
- Ensure that each urinal is separated by a board to increase privacy for the child and draw attention to inappropriate looking (i.e., craning over a board is more obvious than a surreptitious glance).
- Encourage boys to use stalls over urinals.
- Whenever possible do not enter the stall with a child, rather wait outside the stall until the child is finished.
- If you must enter a stall or single bathroom with a very young child, leave the door open.
- When taking young children to the bathroom, instruct but do not touch.
- Provide step-by-step instructions aloud, so that both the child and passerby know what is happening.
- Have caregivers sign a consent form authorizing staff to assist their child with toileting and diapering.

Some churches also adopt a no-diaper-change or no-toileting position wherein if a child needs help with a diaper change, clothing change, or toileting issue, parents are immediately called to help their child. When communicated beforehand to parents, this policy alleviates much of the vulnerability and difficulty inherent in these situations.

Safe Touch

One pastor captures the difficulty of talking about inappropriate touch: one day an older child ran up to him in public and gave him a hug that lasted more than a few seconds. The pastor wanted to show the child affection but also felt unease and uncertainty. Was this hug appropriate? Another pastor, unsure whether she should allow children to sit on her lap, expressed a desire to demonstrate care and welcome to children while also modeling safe touch. A Policy that addresses safe touch provides its congregants and staff with much needed direction, navigating extremes that would eliminate any touch (even healthy touch) or would allow any touch (even abusive behavior). Such guidelines enhance adult-child relationships by enabling adults to offer children the physical interaction they crave, with the confidence that such touch is helpful to the child.

Guidelines for safe touch are important because rarely do caregivers catch child abusers actively abusing, but they commonly observe them engaging in precursors to the abuse, especially physical touch. Individuals who abuse children often commence the abuse with inappropriate touch in order to test tolerance levels for their behavior. These interactions may begin with non-sexual, accidental, or overly physical touch—often in view of others. If bystanders do not notice or challenge the touching, the perpetrator may feel emboldened and push the boundaries further. In order for bystanders to intervene when they observe improper touching, the Policy must delineate between safe and unsafe touches (Chapter Eight addresses Policy violations and bystander intervention).

The Policy should name and prohibit unsafe touch while also naming and promoting safe touch. Churches will have to discuss and determine what constitutes these two categories. Unsafe touch must at least include any sexual and physical abuse as defined in Chapter One. Churches may wish to include specific examples. For example, tapping a child's bottom, even over clothes, should be prohibited. Church staff and volunteers should not use physical force, spanks, or any other form of corporal punishment to control or discipline children. Churches may need assistance in applying the sexual and physical abuse definitions to their specific context and are encouraged to contact their GRACE Certification Specialist or another child protection expert for guidance.

Specifically, the Policy must require touch to be observable and interruptible. The Policy might ask staff and volunteers: are they comfortable telling a caregiver or supervisor about the touch? Does the child want the touch? If no, the adult should not be touching the child. Are they ashamed of or hiding the touch? Is the touch a secret? Are they lying about the touch? If yes, the adult should not be touching the child. Touch that violates social norms or touch that has the appearance of abusive touch is also unsafe and should also be prohibited.

Beyond these prohibitions, it is difficult to categorize touch, since touch that is appropriate in one setting may not be appropriate in another, especially depending upon the age of children. Your church must consider the various contexts where you welcome children and craft guidelines that are appropriate. Touch that is intended to groom a child for abuse may be indistinguishable from healthy, safe touch intended to comfort a child. Despite this difficulty, it is important for your church to specify which touches are off-limits.

The Policy can also note that limiting touch in no way results in limited affection. Warmth can be conveyed by a light touch on the shoulder, a high five, or a side hug. Your church would be wise to include these and other examples of safe and healthy touching alongside the list of unsafe touch.

Churches should also be aware that children who have been victims of sexual abuse may sometimes demonstrate inappropriate sexual or intimate touch (e.g., straddling an adult). If a child attempts to touch an adult in this manner, the adult should gently block the child's attempt and redirect the touching. Depending on the circumstances and the behavior, it may also be appropriate for the adult to seek guidance from a trained professional (e.g., GRACE Certification Specialist, pediatrician, mental health professional, Child Advocacy Center).

An Example of One Church's Rules for Touch*

Examples of Unacceptable Touch

- Sexually or physically abusive touch
- Touching a child's thighs, stomach, or back
- Corporal punishment
- Any touch that is unwanted by a child
- Any touch that is secret
- Touch that sexually gratifies the adult in any way
- Lap sitting
- Tickling
- Playing with hair
- Full frontal hugs
- Tapping a child's clothed bottom

Examples of Acceptable Touch

- Sitting side by side
- High fives, fist bumps, special handshakes
- Side hugs
- Pats on the shoulder
- Carrying a small child on your hip

The above list reflects the rules of one church. Each church will need to create their own list that fits their community.

Extra Attention

In every church, there will be several children who require extra attention: a child with a learning disability, a child who has recently lost a caregiver, a new child who struggles to make friends. Often, the children who need extra attention are also the children who are most vulnerable to abuse.[3] Youth staff and volunteers should be encouraged to meet the varying and individualized needs of the church's children. Because abusers often provide gifts or special treatment to a child in order to gain that child's trust, the Policy should delineate appropriate extra attention from inappropriate preferential attention. Likewise, the Policy should clearly ban favoritism.

The Policy should explicitly state that secret gifts and attention are not allowed. In cases of abuse, preferential treatment is part of the perpetrator's process of grooming a potential victim for future abuse, and the perpetrator usually asks the child to keep gifts or attention a secret. Furthermore, the Policy should prohibit displays of favoritism to a child or group of children, as favoritism excludes other children. Instead, your church should focus upon including and welcoming all children.

If a child needs extra attention, it must be observable and interruptible. To maintain accountability, the Policy may stipulate that special attention and gifts are coordinated in a rotation whereby staff and volunteers take turns providing the extra attention. Gifts should be from the church instead of from individual staff members or volunteers. Whenever staff members plan on giving a gift to or spending special time with a child, they should alert a supervisor or colleague and the child's caregiver. Requiring supervisors to oversee preferential treatment allows them to drop in unexpectedly and reevaluate its necessity.

Furthermore, special attention and gifts should meet a child's need, not an adult's need. To differentiate between safe and unsafe behaviors, a supervisor should check to make certain the staff member can clearly articulate an important reason for the extra attention (e.g., it's the child's birthday, anniversary of a loved one's passing, etc.). However, beware that child abusers are adept at hiding their true motives. Be leery of preferential treatment or special gifts that are more about the adult than the child.

Precautionary Measures for Consideration in Instances of Preferential Treatment

- Staff should be able to articulate a clear reason for providing extra attention to a child.
- Staff should alert a supervisor of their intention to provide extra attention to a child. In cases where there is no supervisor (e.g., the staff member is the head pastor), staff should alert a colleague of the plan and request assistance in implementing these precautions.
- When possible, supervisors might organize a rotation of staff and volunteers so that extra attention is provided by multiple individuals.
- Staff providing extra attention must always abide by the Policy (e.g., meet in public, observable spaces, etc.).
- Supervisors should drop by unexpectedly during outings or meetings.
- Supervisors should periodically reevaluate the situation to determine if extra attention is still necessary.
- Supervisors should make certain to alert their own supervisors about the need for continued oversight of instances of preferential treatment, before resigning from their church role.

Sexual Language and Media

In one youth-serving organization, a staff member would publicly make-out with his wife when she dropped by youth events. At other times, he would joke around with the male youth leaders and share intimate details regarding his sexual life. The organization later discovered that he sexually abused some boys in the youth group. Instead of dismissing inappropriate sexual talk as mere jokes, churches can recognize how boundary violations that involve sexual language set the stage for sexual abuse. As with inappropriate touching, perpetrators often test the waters with relatively minor infractions, and if no one intervenes at this initial stage, they escalate. Even when lewd language and behavior merely reflect normal sexual curiosity—which is often the case with older children— permitting such behavior in the church, or at church-sanctioned events, contributes to an unsafe youth environment.

Language

The Policy should prohibit sexually suggestive language including racy jokes, sexual innuendo, remarks about a person's dress or body, discussion of sexual habits, showing a child pornography, music with sexually explicit lyrics, etc. Sexual language may harm children's development at best, and at worst, is abusive.

The Policy may distinguish between sexually suggestive language, which should be prohibited, and genuine conversations or questions about sex and the body that older children initiate or staff carefully plan and implement. While lewd comments and jokes can create an unsafe youth environment, age-appropriate conversations about sex, physical development, and personal safety are essential components of a plan to prevent abuse and foster healthy development in children. In fact, these topics may be of particular interest or concern to older children as their interest in sex and romantic relationships emerges.

If the church staff or volunteers want to give a lecture or organize a program to help children understand age-appropriate questions about their body or sexuality, the Policy should stipulate that the event be planned in advance. These events should never be a surprise. Parents should have advance notice of the event so they can make an informed choice to send their child and follow up with them after the event, or they may choose to keep their child home from the event. Parents and church leadership should always be welcome at such events.

If children have impromptu questions about their bodies or sexuality, keep the conversation age-appropriate, offer as few details as possible, and stay on the topic initiated by the child. In a spirit of maintaining transparency, the staff member or volunteer should inform their supervisor of the conversation. Together, they can decide whether parents should be informed of the conversation as well.

Media

Your church will have to decide how to handle media, video games, and music that have sexual themes. At a minimum, the Policy must explicitly prohibit adults from showing children any form of pornography because anytime an adult shows a child pornography, this is abuse. Similarly, the Policy should prohibit movies with sex scenes, video games with sexual violence, or any sexually explicit media images. Ensuring compliance with the Policy with regard to music, movies, and video games will require youth departments to plan in advance. One pastor learned this lesson the hard way, as he accepted a movie recommendation without watching it first. He showed the movie at a fourth and fifth grade event, and the movie opened with a sexual act. The sexually explicit materially was clearly inappropriate, and the pastor should have previewed the movie. An advanced screening would have prevented the situation.

How does your church use media and how can it help the youth department to avoid inappropriate sexual themes? The Policy may require the youth department to preview movies, make playlists for music, have caregivers approve video games in the youth rooms, or prohibit teachers from using PG-13 and R-rated movies as illustrations for their lessons. However your church's youth department uses media, think of creative ways to ensure that sexually inappropriate messages do not sneak into the programming. One situation that needs particular advanced planning is when children travel for youth department events. The Policy should stipulate that youth departments will contact hotels and ask them to shut down the pornography available through the hotel's television or pay-per-view services.

Technology and Social Media

With regard to technology, all the previously discussed rules for safe behaviors apply whether an adult is interacting with a child in-person or through technology and social media. Whether the staff member or volunteer is connecting with a child at the mall, through SnapChat, the park, or an online game world, their behavior must fully comply with the Policy. For example, online interactions should meet the best practice of having two adults present or being observable and interruptible. The interactions should never be secret. When interacting on social media, interact publicly, not through private messages. Similarly, when texting, it is best to text the child and the parent or use a texting app that allows others to see the text.

Likewise, words and interactions should comply with all the standards of speech, avoiding any sexual language. If volunteers or staff members text with students, they should include parents in the text or ask parents for permission to text with their child. Any private texts should also be procedural—confirming time and places for youth group, etc.

Photographs or videos of children should not be posted any-where, including on bulletin boards, fliers, newsletters, church web-sites, or social media/photo-sharing sites (e.g., Google +, Instagram, Flickr, Snapfish, Picasa, Facebook, Twitter, Snapchat, Pinterest, etc.), without written permission from the caregiver and child.[4] A simple means for procuring that permission is to include an opt-in box on the youth registration form regarding picture posting. (Reg-istration will be discussed in Chapter Seven.) The Policy should also explicitly prohibit photos of children who are unclothed, toileting, changing clothes, in swimwear, or wet. Churches can then create password-protected photo albums on their youth department web-sites where they can post pictures from youth events of children for whom they already have written permission. Avoid giving out their full names, schools, names of friends, or other information that gives away their location.

Policy Worksheet: Interactive Guidelines
---

1. This guide suggests having at least two, unrelated adults supervising all youth activities.

Sample Policy Language:

> Because most child abuse happens in isolated situations and because most adults seeking to harm a child prefer to do so in private, our church requires two, unrelated adults to supervise all youth events, including but not limited to …

What you would add to the statement for your context?

What would you take away?

2. List all church activities where children are present:

»

»

»

»

»

3. Place a check mark by all events that should have two adults supervising at all times.

4. Which events in your list are harder to have two adults supervising? Underline these.

5. Of the events that are underlined, based upon the criteria set forth in this chapter, what events should the Policy prohibit? Put an X through those events.

6. Because some events, such as mentoring, require one adult to focus attention on one child, include a statement requiring interactions to be interruptible and observable.

Sample Policy Language:

> The more an interaction is observable and interruptible, the better. When adults spend time with a child, the adults will inform both the child's caregiver and their supervisor of each meeting. The adult and child will meet at a time and place where the caregiver or supervisor can interrupt the time or observe the time from a distance. Furthermore, the meeting will take place at a public place with high visibility.

7. Fill out the following chart with your remaining, underlined events. Put the event on the left side of the chart, and on the right side, list ways that the event can become observable, interruptible, and safer. Include the chart in your Policy.

Potential One-on-One Adult-Child Interactions	Safety Suggestions

8. The guide suggests distinguishing between acceptable and unacceptable touch between adults and children in a church setting.

Sample Policy Language:

[Faith Church] prohibits the following:

- » Sexually or physically abusive touch
- » Touching a child's thighs, stomach, or back
- » Corporal punishment
- » Any touch that is unwanted by a child
- » Lap sitting
- » Tickling
- » Playing with hair
- » Full frontal hugs

What would your church add to this list?

- »
- »
- »
- »

Sample Policy Language:

[Faith Church] desires to show healthy affection to its children through the following:

- » Displays of affection that are observable and interruptible
- » Kind words
- » High fives
- » Pats on the shoulder
- » Side hugs

What would you add to this list?

- »
- »
- »

Extra Attention

Sample Policy Language:

»   Staff are prohibited from displaying favoritism toward a
    child or group of children.

»   Staff may not give gifts to individual children unless the
    gifts are:

    ⁓   Able to be given to other children at other times for
        similar reasons (e.g., gifts to graduating seniors; a new
        Bible for students entering middle school; end of the
        year thank-you gifts to older children who volunteered
        in the nursery)

    ⁓   Signed from the church rather than the individual
        staff member

    ⁓   Given together with another staff member

    ⁓   A personal gift from a staff member that meets
        social expectations and does not signify preferential
        treatment

»   In cases where staff believe that a child would benefit from
    extra attention:

    ⁓   Staff should be able to articulate a clear reason for
        providing extra attention to a child that focuses on the
        child's needs, not staff needs.

    ⁓   Staff must receive authorization from a supervisor
        before providing extra attention to a child. In cases
        where there is no supervisor (e.g., the staff member is a
        senior pastor), staff should alert a colleague of the plan
        and request that the colleague function in the role of a
        supervisor.

    ⁓   When possible, supervisors might organize a rotation
        of staff and volunteers so that extra attention is not
        provided solely by one individual.

- ~ Staff providing extra attention must always abide by the Policy (e.g., meet in observable and interruptible spaces).
- ~ Supervisors should occasionally drop by unexpectedly during outings or meetings.
- ~ Supervisors should periodically reevaluate the situation to determine if extra attention is still necessary.

For your context, what would you add?

Strike through any suggestions that do not fit your context.

Sexual Language

Sample Policy Language:

[Faith Church] acknowledges that sexual language is more than mere jokes, but a serious boundary violation. As such, the following are prohibited:

» Sexually suggestive language, racy jokes, sexual innuendo, descriptions of sexual experiences/habits
» Uploading, downloading, or viewing of pornography
» Music, videos games, and movies with sexual themes

If the church staff or volunteers want to give a lecture or organize a program to help youth understand age-appropriate questions about their body or sexuality, the event must be planned in advance and parents notified beforehand. When children or teens raise questions about their body or sexuality, [Faith Church] volunteers and staff will answer the question at hand in an age-appropriate way and inform a supervisor.

[Faith Church] encourages positive verbal interactions, including:

- » Encouragement
- » Kind words
- » Positive reinforcement
- » Appropriate jokes

Strike through any language that does not fit your church's context.

What would you add for your church's context?

CHAPTER SEVEN

· · · ·

ROUTINE PROTECTIVE MEASURES

Beyond an individual's behavior, communities have routines that can either contribute to children's safety or expose them to vulnerable situations. Drop-off and pick-up times at nursery and children's classes, for example, present many challenges to safeguarding children. Pick-up times are often crowded and chaotic. Perpetrators can take advantage of this routine. In one church, a two-year-old's cousin picked him up from nursery, and this cousin had a restraining order not to have contact with the child. Without a drop-off Policy to guide them, the workers saw that the child recognized the man and released the child into the cousin's care, assuming he was the father. A minute later, the child's mother arrived, expecting to find her child. Immediately, the mother recognized that someone else had picked up her child. The mother and workers raced after the boy and found the cousin leading the child into a car. Thankfully, the mother intervened.

A Policy that clearly defines drop-off and pick-up procedures could have possibly saved this mother and child a traumatic experience. In many cases, children are easily accessible at the church. However, the church can take measures to offset that vulnerability and support any protective orders or special circumstances families may have. Consider how your church functions when children are received at the beginning of a program and released after the program. In addition, there are other security issues that churches must address. How is your building security managed? Who has keys and are they screened? What happens when rooms and sections of the building are not being used? The following chapter explores these situations and how to account for child protection during those times.

Registration

Registering children for church events gives staff and volunteers the information they need about a particular child to care for that child well. What is the child's preferred name? Does the child have an allergy? Is there a book that calms a child at drop-off for nursery? Who is allowed to take the child from an event? These, and more, are all valid questions that a registration process can answer. Once parents or caregivers register their children, taking attendance and responding to emergencies also becomes easier.

At the beginning of each year, churches can create a registration list that includes each child's name, contact information, best number to reach parents or caregivers during church events, allergies, and other special needs. The registration should also designate who is allowed to pick up the child. Think through your church's schedule. What other information would be helpful for children's workers to have in an emergency? Registration should be required as a prerequisite for attending events where a child is left with church staff or volunteers. There is software available to churches that can facilitate this process.

Having this information readily available allows staff to respond appropriately in the event of an emergency (e.g., medical, evacuation, or lost child) because it requires parents to inform the church of the children's needs and because it records the children's attendance at a particular event. The church has a responsibility to know where each participating child is throughout the entire time that child is in its care, an impossible task if the church does not know which children are in attendance. Furthermore, if a child were to be harmed during an event, staff would waste precious time trying to find parents or caregivers and obtain important medical and personal information. Registering children records their presence at a particular event and keeps pertinent information about them readily available to youth leaders.

At first, this registration process may feel unwelcoming to guests or to unregistered children. Protecting children and creating hospitable communities can feel at odds with each other, but there are creative ways to overcome this difficulty. Consider ways to incorporate both the necessary child protection protocols and a welcoming environment for guests. For example, churches that are uncomfortable turning away unregistered children could create a guest pass for out-of-town visitors or a set number of unregistered "trial" visits for in-town residents who forget to register. They may designate a volunteer to greet guests and help them with the registration process. These options allow the church to practice child protection while also practicing warm hospitality. Furthermore, as churches prioritize children's safety, the culture of our immediate and extended Christian communities will change. As the practice becomes routine, it will feel more hospitable.

Once a child's attendance is recorded for an event, it is the church's responsibility to supervise those children from the time they are dropped off until the time they are picked up.

Pick-up

Dismissal from events can be crowded and chaotic, and the Policy should stipulate appropriate procedures to guide staff and volunteers. Without protocols to guide the process, there is a greater likelihood that staff and volunteers will make split-second judgments that might be inaccurate or unsafe. In the mildest of scenarios, allowing someone other than a caregiver or designated caregiver to pick up a child can lead to a wild goose chase, confusion, or even panic when the caregiver comes to retrieve the child, and she is not there. More seriously, it allows for the possibility that another congregant or family member seeking to harm a child may pick up the child and claim to be doing the caregiver a favor. It also permits a stranger to walk in off the street and pretend to be a friend or relative of a family in order to gain access to a child for abusive purposes.

Churches will want to prohibit the release of a child to anyone other than the caregiver without express, advance permission. While this rule can certainly be cumbersome, the severity of the worst-case scenario warrants any inconvenience to families or church staff. During registration, churches can ask families who is allowed to pick up their child to make the process easier on them.

Depending upon the church, the Policy may also have an appropriate age at which children may come and go on their own.[1] For example, a church may require parents to pick up their elementary school aged children from church events, but after certain events, middle school students may be released on their own to find their parents in the church building. Children beneath the determined age who wish to leave an event before its dismissal time should be accompanied by a youth department staff member until the staff releases the child into an approved person's care.

Building Security

When protecting children, churches must consider their church's physical structure. Pay particular attention to hidden, isolated, or unsupervised areas where someone seeking to harm a child would have an opportunity to do so. In one church, two young sisters were unsupervised and playing alone in a classroom when a man entered and abused them both. If the church had that classroom locked, the sisters may have been spared this traumatic experience. There are two basic ways to overcome vulnerable areas in the building, by careful design of the physical space and by utilizing supervision.

Designing a space that prioritizes children's safety means restricting access to certain areas as well as increasing visibility in others. A church must decide which spaces are off limits and which are accessible to children. If children customarily play in the church's unsupervised lobby or office spaces, offenders can easily take advantage of this routine. Churches can reduce this risk by designating spaces for children to play and locking areas where children should not be.

If a room or area within the church is not in use at a given time (e.g., closets), the Policy should require these spaces be locked so that they cannot serve as private space for any type of abuse. Because room usage changes with the programming, locking unused rooms should become a routine part of coordinating an event or regular service. Depending on your church's facility, the Policy may want to stipulate locking offices on Sunday or locking an unused main sanctuary during the week. Think through the physical structures on your property and ensure that all buildings and spaces within church premises that are not required for services cannot be accessed.

In addition to restricting access, churches can use design features to increase visibility in areas where children are allowed. Depending on the church's structures, the Policy can increase visibility through adding windows or two-way mirrors in doors and maintaining proper lighting.

By ensuring that all doors have windows or two-way mirrors, caregivers and supervisory staff can easily see what is happening in the classroom at all times. A church without windows in its doors should consider investing in their installation or leaving the door partially open.[2] Youth directors who wish to block the windows in order to avoid distraction in the classrooms should make sure that the coverings (e.g., curtains or shades) are installed on the outside of the windows. This ensures that caregivers and supervisors have the option of unobtrusively peeking in.

Ensuring that all children and youth areas have proper lighting is another method of increasing visibility. Consider all areas of the church, including classrooms, stairwells, and hallways. Does each space have adequate lighting? Could someone passing by easily see into that space? If not, add overhead lighting or lamps to the area.

Having a child protection expert conduct a property inspection to identify vulnerable areas and possibilities for overcoming those vulnerabilities may be helpful to your church. Churches participating in the GRACE Child Safeguarding Certification have this inspection included in their certification process. Your community's child protection center may also offer this service.

Security Personnel

Along with building security, personnel supervision can help manage vulnerable areas within the church. Because of differing geographic locations, financial resources, and values, churches vary in the amount and type of supervision they choose to implement. Some churches may retain professional security guards, some may recruit volunteer "greeters" from the congregation, some may install security cameras that are continuously monitored, and some may choose a combination.

In churches that have professional security personnel, a guard may be positioned at the entrance to the building and/or at the entrance to the youth wing. Because paid security guards may have other duties beyond protecting children, educate the guards about the risk of child sexual abuse posed from within the building and require all security guards to be trained in the Policy and child abuse dynamics. Security guards must be held to the safe behaviors outlined in Chapter Six and be screened thoroughly.

Churches may also wish to establish and implement a roster for two congregants to walk the church grounds and keep an eye out for children who are not attending the service or a supervised children's program. These volunteers may also spot-check the windows or two-way mirrors in the children's areas. They should also ensure that all rooms that are not in use have been locked. As with the security guards, if churches use congregants in this manner, they should be trained in the Policy, agree to abide by its safe behaviors, and be screened thoroughly.

Security Measures to Consider in Developing a Policy

Design

- Opt for open layouts with maximum visibility when constructing new churches.
- Renovate existing spaces to maximize visibility.
- Ensure that all spaces, particularly those with minimal traffic (e.g., a basement), are well lit.
- Install windows in all doors. When this is not possible, keep doors propped open.
- Consider installing two-way mirrors in walls or doors of any rooms where children will be.
- Consider installing security cameras throughout the church property.

Personnel

- Hire security guards or recruit volunteer greeters. These might be stationed at the entrance to the building or youth wing, and might conduct periodic walk-throughs of the church premises, to ensure that no one is harming a child and that children are not in unsafe spaces.
- Determine which spaces/events are off-limits to adults.
- Designate supervised spaces where it is acceptable for children to spend time.
- Lock all unused and unsupervised spaces.

Policy Worksheet: Routine Protective Measures

Sample Policy Language:

> At the beginning of each ministry year, [Faith Church] will create a registration for any child who attends activities and programs. The registration will record who may safely pick-up a child from an event and other helpful information about the child. Attendance will be taken at all events. Once a child's attendance is recorded for an event, it is the church's responsibility to supervise those children from the time they are dropped off until the time they are picked up by a caregiver.

What information would your church like to ask for in the registration form?

>> Who may pick up a child from a church event
>> Allergy the child has
>> Any medical concerns
>> Doctor to contact in case of an emergency
>>
>>
>>
>>
>>

List the various children's and youth activities and events at your church:

>> Nursery
>>
>>
>>
>>

»

»

Place a check mark by all that will require a parent or caregiver to sign their child out from the event. Underline events where the children are old enough to be released without a parent/caregiver present.

Will your church designate greeters or hire security guards who can help with security? _____ yes _____ no

If yes, what will their responsibilities be?

» Lock unused closets and rooms
» Spot-check classrooms
» Help with visitor registration
»
»

Policy Section Three

Responding to Policy Violations and Child Abuse

"I wish that any of the adults in my life would have protected me . . . a lot of them knew, even my own mother, she just pretended she didn't."

—survivor of child sexual abuse

Considerable time goes into creating a thoughtful, comprehensive Policy to guide your church. These efforts are for good reason, as the Policy is one of your church's best safeguards against child sexual abuse, but for this safeguard to reach its fullest potential in keeping children and the church safe, it needs to be enforced. How seriously a church treats Policy violations and abuse disclosures determines how effective its Policy will be at preventing opportunities for abuse.

It may be helpful to think of the Policy as the perimeter of your community. Dr. Joe Tucci, CEO of the Australian Childhood Foundation, explains this idea well in his summary of the lessons learned from the Australian Royal Commission into Institutional Responses to Child Sexual Abuse,

Potential perpetrators of abuse won't try to abuse a child straight up, but first they will test the perimeter in a small way. It might be something like taking a photo of a child on their phone, and even though it's a breach of policy a fellow staff member thinks it's innocent enough so the perpetrator learns that the perimeter is not strong. . . . Time and again the Royal Commission showed that these small breaches that seem innocuous are actually tests by the perpetrator to see if the response is weak or strong. If it's weak, they'll move to the next test. If it's strong, they might move to the next organisation.[1]

It is the whole congregation's job to keep the perimeter of your church secure. A situation may call for bystander intervention, documenting the event and nothing else, or a church may follow up a Policy violation with further education about the Policy and expectations about safe behavior toward children. When necessary, someone may need to call the legal authorities. In some situations, the church could benefit from enacting a Limited Access Agreement with one of its members—clearly defining a problematic behavior, the expected behavior, and continued accountability. At times, your church may need to seek assistance in the form of an independent review. The following chapters outline when and how to respond to Policy violations, contact the legal authorities, implement a Limited Access Agreement, and seek an independent review. These chapters explore possible responses to various situations. When in doubt about which response is best, consult an expert in child protection for guidance. If your church is participating in the GRACE Child Safeguarding Certification, contact your Certification Specialist for continued assistance.

CHAPTER EIGHT

. . . .

POLICY VIOLATIONS

One of the many benefits of having a Policy is that it highlights potentially concerning behavior and gives churches freedom to intervene early, before the concerning behavior escalates. Violations provide churches with valuable information—they function as indicators of a potentially larger problem. Dr. Tucci clearly articulates the importance of responding well to Policy violations, saying, "We've seen teachers who have been charged with sexual assault of a young person, and that's really the final act. The preparatory or grooming act is often hundreds of texts that engages that young person in a relationship they've kept secret from the family, and it's about socialising the child outside of the classroom."[1]

Each Policy violation will require a different level of response. In some cases, the violation will rise to the level of abuse or suspicion of abuse. If the witnessed Policy violation includes abuse of a child, as defined in Chapter One, the community must act immediately to protect the child. This might mean taking the child away from the scene or remaining at the scene with the child until help arrives. No one who witnesses abuse should ever leave the scene while the child remains unprotected or in the presence of the alleged abuser. Once the child is safe, the next step is to file an external report to the proper authorities (see Chapter Ten on Reporting for detailed instructions) and enact safeguards within the community (see

Chapter Nine on Limited Access Agreements). Chapter Ten also delineates what qualifies as suspicion of abuse.

In most cases, however, the violation will breach a term of the Policy that may seem minor or insignificant, but every Policy violation deserves a response. While churches want to avoid a paranoid culture, they need to remain vigilant to Policy violations. Bystanders can intervene and redirect when an adult displays unsafe behavior. Some policy violations may also need to be documented. In some cases, churches can help people violating the Policy with further education about the Policy or about child abuse dynamics. The following chapter explores these possible responses: bystander intervention, documentation, and further education. Finally, every Policy will have exceptions: times when it is acceptable to break the Policy.

Bystander Intervention

Enforcing the Policy is a community effort requiring everyone's participation. Staff in particular should enforce the Policy just as they enforce any other church policies—calmly and firmly. However, church staff cannot pursue compliance alone. To borrow a line from the US Department of Homeland Security's anti-terrorism campaign, "if you see something, say something." Enforcing the Policy is everyone's obligation.

This message of shared responsibility is especially relevant because early intervention can prevent grooming behavior from escalating to abusive behavior. Individual responses to Policy violations will determine your church's culture around this issue. Do people let the violation slide or is there an immediate redirection from bystanders? An appropriate and immediate response sends a clear message to potential perpetrators: our Policy is not just a formality, but a value the community lives. Churches can cultivate this attitude with well-implemented training as Chapter Fourteen will discuss, but it also requires bystander intervention.

When an individual is seen violating the Policy, bystanders must intervene: the problematic behavior should be named, the Policy rules explained, and the individual redirected toward safer behavior. An example of such a situation would be a volunteer witnessing her co-teacher prepping a movie-clip to use as an illustration during Sunday school, but the clip comes from a movie that is rated R. The clip may be innocent, and the other volunteer may have pure intentions. However, if the church asks its staff and volunteers to refrain from showing clips from movies that have sexual themes, then it is a Policy violation. If you were the bystander, how would you respond? Here is an example:

Bystander:	I noticed this clip is from a movie that has a lot of sexual themes. The clip seems fine, but the Policy says we need to have parental permission to show this.
Volunteer:	Oh, right. I forgot about that. What should we do? I've already prepared for today's class.
Bystander:	Let's come up with another activity to illustrate this lesson. I'd be glad to help. What's the topic?
Volunteer:	Sounds good! The topic is . . .

While this fabricated conversation was easy and smooth, bystander interventions may feel awkward or difficult. To help ease the difficulty, churches can train staff and volunteers in bystander intervention, focus on behavior instead of motive, and educate about safe behaviors.

Bystander intervention is a skill that must be learned. It is not instinctive knowledge. Training on bystander intervention should be made available to everyone in the church. As with the acquisition of any new skill, learning to intervene is most effective when it is taught experientially. Training for staff and congregants should include role-plays where participants have an opportunity to practice intervening. Chapter Fourteen explores topics and methods of training that may benefit your church.

Another key is for the bystander to be prepared and to intervene calmly, naming the behavior without questioning the violation's motives. Bystander intervention does not call for judgment of the individual violating the Policy. It is simply a matter of acting to ensure the Policy is followed, regardless of the violator's intent.

People might violate the Policy because

- they don't know it exists
- they are unaware of a particular term
- they misunderstood a particular term
- they disagree with a particular term
- the Policy is new, and they are not yet used to its new terms
- they are actively grooming a child for future abuse
- they have already harmed a child, and this violation is part of, or indicator of, that harm

Remember when someone sees a Policy violation, any of the previously mentioned motivations could be at play. It is not the bystander's job to determine another's motives. Instead, Policy violations are best viewed as opportunities to educate and redirect than as intentional noncompliance. Sometimes individuals violate a Policy because they are unaware that it exists. As previously discussed, Policy dissemination and training helps. However, some people will always be out of the loop or not knowledgeable of all the terms. Other individuals might know of the Policy but disagree or not understand (imagine the elderly congregant who does not understand the need to check with parents before giving candy to a child). Intervening and redirecting in these situations without over-reacting helps to shift the culture of the church, reinforce the Policy, and minimize the opportunities for abuse to occur. Bystander intervention guards children without causing undue disruption to ongoing programs or needlessly embarrassing someone for an innocent mistake or outmoded belief.

Documentation

How much churches choose to document Policy violations will greatly vary from church to church. Tailoring the process of documentation is important as every church has its own system of communication, level of organization, and cultural expectations. Some churches may decide to document for particular violations that they define beforehand. (See Appendix Two for a sample.) These churches may find extensive documentation too cumbersome or extreme. Documenting too often or invasively may feel more like paranoia instead of protection. These churches may designate which behaviors and which violations warrant further documentation and which do not.

Other churches may choose to document every Policy violation, asking staff and volunteers to fill out an Incident Report anytime they use bystander intervention. In these churches, whenever anyone has to practice bystander intervention, the bystander should document the incident and give the documentation to the church leadership. The church leadership can add this form to the individual's file. Then, churches can review any previous incidents reported. A sample *Incident Report* form is available in Appendix Two, but churches can adjust this form or create their own. Anything that makes communicating easier is good.

Churches that choose to document often may find that recording and filing violations enables the church to identify patterns or repeat violations. In churches where there is high turnover or a large membership—meaning that many different people may have noticed Policy violations by a particular individual—documenting more frequently may be helpful. Documentation also helps when dealing with offenders who test the perimeter more than once, but strategically space the tests out over time, making the pattern difficult to detect. It is important for a church that decides to document all violations to develop a manner of doing so that does not create an environment that fosters paranoia or provides too much control to a select few within the church.

In some cases, bystander intervention may be all the situation requires. In other cases, a more serious response is warranted. To determine if an individual's behavior requires more response, the church should review its documentation. Try filling out the following chart. It can sometimes be difficult to recognize a pattern or serious concern until it is laid out in a list format.

	Date	Policy violations/ Concerning behavior	Response of bystanders/ staff to the behavior
1			
2			
3			
4...			

One church was notified about an individual who was making other members uncomfortable. They were prepared to dismiss the behavior as *weird but not concerning*, until they engaged in this exercise and realized that there were nineteen instances of concerning boundary violations spanning a period of fifteen years. Viewed collectively, these behaviors clearly warranted a response.

Once a church has reviewed the documentation, they may respond as necessary. Instances requiring an escalated response might include a pattern of grooming behavior, where the individual behaviors themselves appear to be innocuous. Such instances could also include where a person demonstrates a low regard for the Policy by engaging in consistent minor policy violations. Furthermore, a single, more serious violation also warrants an escalated response, such as covering a door window when meeting with a child or showing excessive or secret attention to a vulnerable child. Churches will have to define for themselves what warrants a more serious violation. If churches have any questions or concerns about whether they should follow up with an individual, it is always a good idea to consult with a child protection expert. If your church is going through the GRACE Child Safeguarding Certification, then contact your Certification Specialist as multiple or more serious Policy violations arise.

Whether there's a pattern of smaller violations or a single, serious violation, it is time to move to escalate the response, which includes meeting with the individual and setting clear limits.

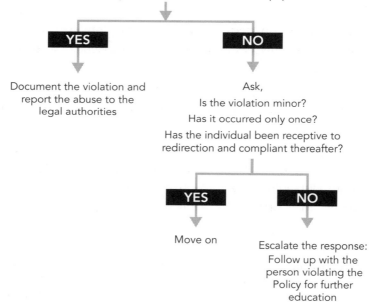

Does the violation fit the legal definition of sexual, emotional, or physical abuse?

Does the violation raise suspicion of sexual, emotional, or physical abuse?

YES

NO

Document the violation and report the abuse to the legal authorities

Ask,

Is the violation minor?

Has it occurred only once?

Has the individual been receptive to redirection and compliant thereafter?

YES

NO

Move on

Escalate the response: Follow up with the person violating the Policy for further education

Further Education

Once the church becomes aware that a congregant has engaged in behavior that requires an escalated response, a meeting needs to be scheduled with the congregant as soon as possible. Sometimes church members have all sorts of meetings among themselves, but rarely take the time to speak directly to the individual in question. Without meeting directly with the person whose behavior is in question, churches may miss important information, allow the behavior to grow, or miss out on a valuable educational moment with the congregant. The purpose of the meeting is not to adjudicate the merits of the reported violation, but to simply notify individuals that the church has been made aware of instances in which they have allegedly engaged in unsafe behaviors or violations of the Policy and to educate about the Policy and the community's expected behavior toward children. Because abuse thrives on secrecy, speaking openly about the Policy violations and unsafe behaviors will either educate a person who had no intention of hurting a child or place a potential offender on notice that he is being watched and help to minimize his opportunities to abuse.

8 Suggestions for Conducting a Meeting with an Individual Observed to Engage in Risky Behaviors

1. List the specific instances of inappropriate/unsafe behaviors or Policy violations.
2. Following Step 1, be quiet and allow the individual time to respond. Sometimes an individual will admit to these and/or other offenses, while in other instances the individual might lie or shift blame to the child.
3. Explicitly state that the behavior is concerning and explain why it puts children at risk.
4. If no abuse is disclosed, give the individual an opportunity to correct his behavior. Validate any service the individual has provided to the community and explain that this meeting is also meant to protect him (i.e., his reputation).
5. Review the rules of the Policy.
6. Ask the individual to agree in writing to abide by the Policy and any additional rules communicated to him at the meeting. Provide a copy of the document (and Policy) to the individual, and retain a copy for the church.
7. Inform the individual that specific people will be following up with him to ensure that he abides by the agreement.
8. Reassure the individual that as long as he upholds his end of the agreement he will be warmly welcomed in the church. Provide specific examples of healthy, appropriate ways for him to engage in church life.

After the meeting, church leaders should debrief to document the meeting and determine next steps. Beyond documentation, no further action may be necessary. If the church leaders are satisfied with the individual's response (e.g., he expresses appreciation for the seriousness of the violation and promises to reform his behavior), they should summarize the discussion, and any agreements reached in the meeting, in a confirmatory writing between the parties. The church may feel that they need to provide continued accountability to ensure the person abides by the policy. If so, the church leaders should assign a few specific people who will follow up with the individual to ensure compliance. If the church feels even more accountability is necessary, they may consider a Limited Access Agreement, which is discussed in Chapter Nine.

Such meetings, again, are for individuals whose violations do not rise to the level of abuse or suspicion of abuse. If the individuals' actions are abusive or if the pattern of violation leads the church to suspect abuse, then report the abuse to the legal authorities. Do not meet with the individual. Furthermore, such meetings are not for staff members or official volunteers. There is no justification for a staff member repeatedly to violate the Policy. Due to the fact that staff and official volunteers will have previously acknowledged reviewing the policy and agreeing to abide by it, any policy violation by a staff member or official volunteer should be grounds for formal discipline, including and up to, termination of employment.

FOLLOWING THE MEETING, ASK

Has your meeting given you cause for increased concern?

Has the individual continued to violate the policy?

Is there a suspicion of child abuse?

Is there an allegation of child abuse?

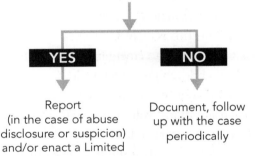

YES	NO
Report (in the case of abuse disclosure or suspicion) and/or enact a Limited Access Agreement	Document, follow up with the case periodically

Policy Exceptions

Everyone in the church—employees, volunteers, and congregants—has an obligation to abide by the Policy. This is as true for the child-care volunteer as it is for the prominent board member. When churches make exceptions or look the other way for certain people, they have neutralized the protective force of the Policy.

There will, however, be times when Policy exceptions need to be made for practical or programmatic reasons. Sometimes when churches draft a Policy, they worry about all the far-fetched possibilities that might arise that would make a specific term too limiting. Getting caught up in all the permutations of a particular rule will make it impossible for churches to progress. Instead, churches need to legislate for the routine programmatic realities but include a general clause regarding emergencies and exceptions to those rules. Doing so allows the churches to take the rules and their enforcement seriously while still accommodating for reality.

Policy exceptions should always be kept to a minimum; however, if a church allows Policy exceptions, these should fall into two categories: emergencies and preapproved exceptions. Furthermore, all exceptions, whether preapproved or an emergency, should also be documented.

Emergencies

Responses to emergency situations often require a deviation from the Policy terms; this is okay. Churches will need to define for themselves what constitutes an emergency. Generally, an emergency is a situation where children's physical health is at risk and violating the Policy would be safer for the children involved than following the Policy. In such situations, volunteers, staff, and church members must do whatever is necessary to keep everyone safe in the moment. For example, a Policy should prohibit staff from giving children rides in their vehicles as this is an isolated, one-on-one environment. However, during one church's children's program, a child had a medical emergency. Because an ambulance would not arrive for twenty minutes and the child needed immediate medical care, an adult drove the child to the hospital in ten minutes. The adults responding to this situation had the freedom to seek the necessary medical care for the child. Even though they violated the Policy, these adults were right to drive the child to the hospital.

As soon as possible, the adult handling the emergency should alert the parents and any necessary church staff. After the emergency has passed, the adult should record the incident, explaining why it was necessary to deviate from the Policy. A sample form is available in Appendix Two.

Preapproved Exceptions

When volunteers or staff members are planning a youth event, they may occasionally request an exception to the Policy. Such exceptions should be thought through in advance and approval should be sought from appropriate church leadership well before the event in question. The litmus test for whether an exception should be made is whether the staff, volunteers, or members can clearly articulate a reason that makes the exception to the policy absolutely necessary, and how they can keep children safe despite the violation. If they can, do what you need to do to keep the children safe: document the violation, ensure caregivers are aware of the situation, and communicate it to the church leadership. See the sample form in Appendix Two.

Policy Worksheet: Policy Violations

Sample Policy Language:

[Faith Church] takes Policy violations seriously. Any staff, volunteer, parent, or church member who witnesses a violation is expected to respond in an appropriate way. [Faith Church] expects all adults to practice bystander intervention when they see a Policy violation. Church leaders will respond according to the following:

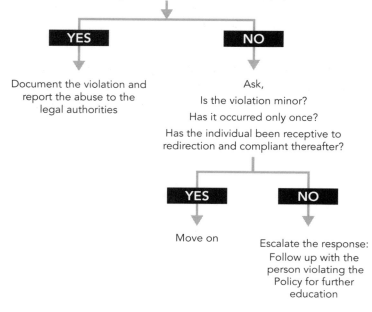

LOOKING AT THE DOCUMENTATION, FIRST ASK

Does the violation fit the legal definition of sexual, emotional, or physical abuse?

Does the violation raise suspicion of sexual, emotional, or physical abuse?

YES

Document the violation and report the abuse to the legal authorities

NO

Ask,
Is the violation minor?
Has it occurred only once?
Has the individual been receptive to redirection and compliant thereafter?

YES

Move on

NO

Escalate the response: Follow up with the person violating the Policy for further education

Has your meeting given you cause for increased concern?

Has the individual continued to violate the policy?

Is there a suspicion of child abuse?

Is there an allegation of child abuse?

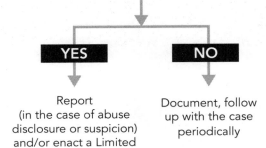

YES

Report
(in the case of abuse
disclosure or suspicion)
and/or enact a Limited
Access Agreement

NO

Document, follow
up with the case
periodically

Sample Policy Language: Policy exceptions should be rare. [Faith Church] allows Policy exceptions that are preapproved or for emergencies. All exceptions should be documented.

CHAPTER NINE

. . . .

LIMITED ACCESS AGREEMENTS

Abuse thrives on secrecy, but transparency and accountability help to counteract secrecy, prevent abuse, and promote safety. One way churches can pursue transparency and accountability is through Limited Access Agreements for individuals who engage in concerning or risky behavior around children. A Limited Access Agreement is a written and agreed-upon boundary between an individual and a community wherein a community outlines its specific concerns about an individual's behavior, details appropriate behavior toward children, and plans ongoing accountability for the individual. Community members who have engaged in repeated, minor Policy violations or have engaged in risky behavior that could put children at risk (e.g., any form of abuse defined in this guide, driving under the influence, drug use, etc.) may sometimes require Limited Access Agreements.

In one church, a man named Dan made parents uncomfortable by showing excessive interest in their children, distributing unsolicited gifts, and stroking their children's faces and bodies in a concerning manner. The church met with Dan and explained to him that he was violating their Policy that prohibited touching children in that manner. Dan admitted that he had difficulty maintaining boundaries around children and agreed to abide by the Policy and stop his concerning behavior toward the children. After a couple of weeks, he was back to his concerning behaviors. The church leaders met with Dan a second time, and again Dan agreed to abide by the Policy. This time, however, the church insisted on memorializing the agreement with a Limited Access Agreement. When Dan refused to sign a written agreement, he was asked to leave the church, and the church alerted other churches in the area. When Dan sought membership at another church, they made the same demand: his attendance was contingent on a written agreement that he keep his distance from children. Through a Limited Access Agreement, these churches were able to pursue transparency about the behavior that is expected around their children and to enforce that behavior with appropriate accountability.

Limited Access Agreements apply to members of a church community. They do not apply to known offenders or church staff members. If a convicted offender wants to join the church's community, contact a child protection expert or a GRACE Certification Specialist to help assess the situation in determining the wisest course of action. Similarly, if a person has a credible accusation of child abuse against them—either past or present—but has not been convicted, contact an expert to help assess the situation. If your church is a part of GRACE's Child Safeguarding Certification, your Certification Specialist will offer guidance. (Chapter Eleven also offers some starting principles on these situations.)

Limited Access Agreements also do not apply to staff members. If a staff member repeatedly or egregiously violates the Policy, the best course of action is to remove that individual from the position and require them to submit to a Limited Access Agreement. Staff members should be exemplary in their compliance and enforcement of the Policy. Churches should refer to Chapter Ten on reporting to determine if they need to also call the authorities.

Reasons for a Limited Access Agreement

The box below includes examples of concerning behaviors where a Limited Access Agreement may be appropriate. These represent a sample of red-flag behaviors and are not exhaustive. Your church will need to determine which behaviors warrant a Limited Access Agreement. In many cases, one incident alone might be insufficient to be concerning, but if part of a larger pattern of behavior, it can be an indicator of an unsafe situation. Keep in mind that there are many situations where a Limited Access Agreement may simply be insufficient to ensure the safety and protection of the children and youth, and the individual may need to be asked to leave the church. That is a decision that must ultimately be made by the leadership in consultation with GRACE or another qualified child protection expert.

Examples of Concerning Behavior

- A young child approaches her parent at church and exclaims, "That man kissed me!" The man overhears the comment and immediately responds, "Yeah, on the hand!" The girl points to her cheek and says "No, he kissed me here!" The immediate defensiveness and lie are concerning.
- An adult seeks out teenagers to speak to after services and strokes their hands and forearms throughout the conversation.
- An adult focuses her attention almost exclusively upon children or youth.
- A man inappropriately inserts himself into activities and conversations related to preteen boys. Examples include: Approaching a boy who is praying beside his father to show him how to "pray correctly;" commenting on boys' new facial hair or changing voice; overhearing an argument between a parent and child and interrupting in order to make sure the parent "properly understands" the child.
- A man caresses children and insists on kisses before giving them candy.
- A woman loiters on the youth floor to console any children who might "miss" their parents.

Examples of Concerning Behavior (continued)

- A man calls a kindergarten girl out of Sunday school to tell her to keep her legs together because he can see her panties, and this is not modest.
- A man has been told by the pastor to stop touching children, but does not do so.
- A mother attends teen events and can be seen hanging out with her teenage son's friends.
- An assistant youth director calls the female teen leaders, "Sweetie," insists on walking them home from Friday night events in order to "protect" them, and makes lewd jokes.

Churches are far more likely to catch someone violating their Policy or engaging in concerning behavior than they are to catch someone sexually abusing a child. Because this is so, it is important to note that Policy violations and concerning behavior may be just the tip of the iceberg and the only indication you will ever have that something is wrong. Even if there is nothing more to the observed behavior than meets the eye, the incident must still be addressed in order to create a safe church environment.

Common Resistance

Churches have good reasons to pursue clear boundaries with people engaging in suspicious or risky behavior; nonetheless, enacting a Limited Access Agreement may initially be met with resistance. This resistance may be a simple misunderstanding, but it may also be the manipulation of a person who wants to harm a child. The following interactions represent common resistance to Limited Access Agreements. Even though Limited Access Agreements may be met with resistance, there are good reasons for pursuing them.

The individual may have exhibited poor judgment, but there was never any improper motivation. Let's not embark on a witch hunt, seeing predators lurking in every corner.

- It is best to avoid engaging in a discussion of an individual's intent. No one can know intent. The Policy frees you from this futile conversation and allows you to focus on behavior. If the behavior violated your Policy, it requires a response.
- Those who abuse children are often in denial that their actions are abusive or harmful. They may think of themselves as good people, or even as individuals who protect children. They often employ significant cognitive distortions and convoluted justifications to convince themselves, and those around them, of their virtue. If you ask them, they may sincerely deny any wrongdoing—because they lack the insight necessary to recognize their own behavior for what it is—abuse.

People make a big deal out of every slight misstep these days. To limit this individual's welcome would be to overreact. Let's all calm down.

- We are calm. Calm enough to know that if we ignore concerning behavior now, it can result in tragedy later. As hard as it is to take action now, it will be infinitely harder to take action later.
- Again, we are not labeling this person an abuser. We are insisting that those who attend our church respect the rules that have been painstakingly created to protect children. When individuals do not follow our Policy, we must help them to do so.

(continued)

Our church is meant to be a welcoming place for all. This includes those who have made "mistakes." Who among us has not sinned?

- Repeatedly violating a Child Protection Policy is not always a mistake. At the very least, it communicates a low regard for boundaries and the policies adopted by the community that are designed to protect children. At the very worst, it communicates a more evil intention.
- We should welcome this individual, but never at the expense of child safety. Let's find ways to support this individual while simultaneously prioritizing child safety. Acceptance and access to children are not the same thing; we can provide one without providing the other.

He has true remorse for his actions. In Christianity, people can repent, and we must accept them. Everyone deserves a second chance.

- Even people who have repented may need further accountability.
- Forgiveness does not mean we ignore troubling past or present behavior.
- Authentic repentance can be demonstrated by an individual accepting the Limited Access Agreement terms and conditions put in place by leadership.

Limited Access Agreement Terms

At a minimum, the Limited Access Agreement will require the individual to thoroughly review the Policy and to agree to follow it. While the Policy is a starting place, churches will need to add more terms, specific to the behavioral concerns of the individual in question. For example, people who have been convicted of crimes that do not involve children may need further boundaries beyond the Policy if they are to work or volunteer around children. If a person has been convicted of a DUI, then a church would want to state explicitly in a Limited Access Agreement that the individual cannot drive youth to/from events. If the conviction involves child maltreatment, consult with your GRACE Certification Specialist; remember Limited Access Agreements are not for convicted offenders.

Possible Terms of a Limited Access Agreement

- Must be accompanied to intergenerational services and programs; may not interact with children or loiter in youth spaces
- May attend adult-only lectures and programs
- Pastoral and hospital visits can occur at the individual's home; in-home pastoral counseling; joining a small group or participating in prayer meetings with adults in the community who do not have children in the home; attending a church without children

The more specific churches can be with its terms, the better, even though Limited Access Agreements will never be able to be exhaustive. For example, should a Limited Access Agreement specify that a person must avoid interactions with children at the church, this would include the individuals agreeing that they will:

- Not go downstairs to the youth floor or attend youth events or programs either on or off church premises
- Use the single-use restroom on the main floor rather than multi-use restrooms downstairs
- Not initiate dialogue with a child or an adult who is standing with a child
- Refrain from touching children

- Refrain from hosting children for meals, lodging, or other events
- Refrain from accepting invitations to meals or lodging where children will be present

At least one person in the church should be assigned to monitor the individual's compliance with the Limited Access Agreement. The monitor should not be related or a close friend to the offender. Any designated monitors should be familiar with the terms of the person's Limited Access Agreement and receive basic training on how to function as a supportive monitor and identify early warning signs of non-compliance, boundary violations, or offending behavior, among other topics.

The Policy should designate that Limited Access Agreements include a timetable for regular (e.g., semi-annually or quarterly) meetings between the congregant, the assigned monitor, and church leaders. In these meetings, the monitor can evaluate the congregant's adherence to the terms of the agreement, address any concerns they, the monitors, or the congregant may have, and revise the agreement as necessary. At these meetings, the church can also terminate the Limited Access Agreement if the individual is not complying with its terms.

Every Limited Access Agreement should be specific as to the consequences for violations. Keep in mind that by the time individuals have a Limited Access Agreement, they have already engaged in ongoing concerning and/or risky behavior that has necessitated the need for the Agreement. Therefore, a violation of the Limited Access Agreement must be viewed by leadership with a great amount of concern and in most cases should result in the individual being removed from the church community.

A church can help with Limited Access Agreement compliance by ensuring that the church members whom are directly affected by it are aware of its terms. The Policy should allow church leadership the discretion to communicate about the Limited Access Agreement as necessary. For example, if a person is not allowed into the children's wing, at a minimum, the church staff and volunteers who run the wing should know. In some cases, the church should share information with the whole congregation that will help parents to better protect their children. The communication should be sympathetic and understanding of concerns that parents or those with a history of concerning behavior may have and provide opportunities for dialogue. In addition, it should clearly prohibit harassment of the individual. If you are unsure about what information to share and with whom, contact your GRACE Certification Specialist for guidance.

Policy Worksheet: Limited Access Agreements

Sample Policy Language:

[Faith Church] utilizes Limited Access Agreements to clarify safe behavior around children for community members who have:

» engaged in concerning or risky behavior
» violated the Policy repeatedly
» offenses that are not related to children (e.g., stealing, drug use, DUI, etc.)
»
»
»
»
»
»

A Limited Access Agreement is a written and agreed-upon boundary between an individual and [Faith Church] wherein we outline specific concerns about an individual's behavior, detail appropriate behavior toward children, and plan ongoing accountability for the individual. Limited Access Agreements apply to members of a church community. They do not apply to known offenders or church staff members.

If a convicted offender wants to join [Faith Church's] community, we will contact our GRACE Certification Specialist (or equivalent child protection expert) on how to best interact with a known sex offender. Similarly, if an individual has been credibly accused of child sexual abuse or any form of child maltreatment but has not yet or was not convicted, we will contact our GRACE Certification

Specialist (or equivalent child protection expert) on how to best proceed.

If a staff member violates the Policy, they will be formally warned and then fired if the violation occurs again.

CHAPTER TEN

· · · ·

REPORTING

The abuse of children is not only a sin, but it is a serious crime. When adults report suspected child abuse to the legal authorities, their report could save a child's life. In contrast, silence about suspected abuse brings incredible harm to victims and emboldens offenders. The authorities should be contacted immediately when a child discloses abuse, child abuse is witnessed, or when signs of abuse are observed. In many states, doing so will fulfill a legal obligation.

One sex offender, who taught in a coed high school, sexually assaulted several of his students. After he abused his first victim, a colleague alerted the school board to rumors about his offending behavior. When confronted, the offender convinced the board that the rumors were a misunderstanding. As a result, they chose not to report the incident. Several years and four victims later, someone reported the teacher to the police, and he was convicted. Reflecting on that time in his life, the offender explained that nothing but a report to law enforcement would have stopped his criminal behavior.

Reporting suspicions of abuse benefits victims by potentially rescuing them from their current abuse.[1] Making a report could help unknown current, former, and future victims whereas failing to report forsakes victims, places future victims in harm's way, and emboldens offenders. Underreporting poses a major risk to children.[2] The notorious case of Jerry Sandusky, a football coach at Penn State University, illustrates the pitfalls of underreporting. Sandusky sexually molested dozens of boys over the course of at least fourteen years.[3] Several adults, from separate institutions, knew of the abuse and either did not report it or took no significant action.[4] Sandusky continued to offend and victims continued to suffer under abuse until his offenses were finally reported to the authorities. What happened at Penn State is not unique.[5] Offenders confidently rely on this silence to escape justice and continue perpetrating abuse against children. A well-formed Policy will provide much-needed guidance about reporting. Therefore, the Policy must address what situations should be reported, who should report, how it should be reported, and what other actions they can take when a report is made.

What Should Be Reported?

Every Policy should clearly identify the circumstances when a report should be made to the authorities. The law generally requires reasonable suspicion of child abuse or neglect to file a report—not knowledge, confirmation, or proof of abuse.[6] Check with your state's laws about what constitutes reasonable suspicion to ensure the Policy fully complies. Generally, suspicion includes but is not limited to a witnessed act of abuse, a child's disclosure of abuse, or signs of abuse in a child. When suspicions arise, adults should make a report instead of investigating the incident themselves. Though the law may direct when certain adults are mandated to report, the Policy should encourage that any and all abuse suspicions should be reported, regardless of whether required to do so by law.

In rare cases, adults may witness abuse. The Policy should direct that before reporting what they witnessed, adults must first ensure the child's safety. Once the child is protected, the abuse must be reported immediately. Likewise, an adult might hear from a friend or another church member who witnessed abuse. Hearing a first-hand witness account of abuse is also a reason to report.

When children disclose abuse, whoever receives the disclosure should report it. Children take a big and scary risk when they disclose abuse. One survey of two thousand children indicated that only 6 percent of those who were sexually victimized reported their abuse to an authority figure of any type.[7] Adults who receive abuse disclosures must respond with skill, including reporting the disclosure to the local authorities.

The Policy should direct that all disclosures of abuse be reported. At times, perpetrators might disclose to another adult that they are abusing a child. A perpetrator's disclosure, just like a child's, must be reported. Similarly, any adult who discloses a suspicion that a child is being abused should have their disclosure reported.

When there is a rumor that a child is being abused, the Policy should direct the church leadership to find and verify the source of the rumor to determine if there is a suspicion of abuse. If so, the matter should be immediately reported to law enforcement. Anytime there are questions or concerns regarding the reporting of abuse suspicions, the Policy should direct the church to consult with their GRACE Certification Specialist or other child advocacy professional. In addition, the ChildHelp National Child Abuse Hotline (800-4-A-CHILD) provides confidential guidance to callers who are considering filing a report. They offer crisis intervention, educational information, and referrals to emergency, social service, and support resources.

The Policy should also direct members of the church community to report egregious or consistent signs of abuse in a child. See Chapter Two for a discussion of what those indicators may include. Remember that many of the indicators for child maltreatment can indicate other possibilities than abuse. If an indicator of sexual abuse is present but no abuse has been disclosed, or if there is otherwise insufficient information to form a reasonable suspicion, call a GRACE Certification Specialist or other child advocacy professional.

Witnessing abuse, receiving an abuse disclosure, or noticing signs of abuse in a child are reasons to report. Reporting child abuse is not making an accusation or rendering a final judgment. Instead, a report asks for legal and child advocacy professionals to evaluate relevant information. A child protection agency will assess the information given in the report. If the agency believes that a report contains sufficient information, they will open a case and begin an investigation. The agency may also decide not to open a case. Knowing that the child protection agency will close a case unless they find evidence of abuse can be encouraging to individuals who are hesitant to report suspicions.

Who Should Report Abuse?

All states designate certain individuals as mandated reporters. The law requires all mandated reporters to report suspicions of abuse, and not reporting is a crime. Your church must check into whom your state mandates to report abuse as this varies state to state.

Whatever your state requires, the Policy should inform all mandated reporters in your church of their legal responsibility and express the church's expectation for their full legal compliance. Mandated reporters who do not fulfill their legal obligations may be subject to criminal prosecution. Furthermore, church staff or volunteers who actively cover up abuse may also be criminally liable for aiding and abetting the alleged perpetrator.

In some cases, mandated reporters may seek help from the church in assessing a situation or filing a report. Because of institutional dynamics, mandated reporters may find counsel from an outside source, such as the National Child Abuse Hotline, more helpful. If mandated reporters seek help from or report their suspicions to the church, these actions do not fulfill their legal obligations.

Mandated reporters maintain their individual, legal obligation to report reasonable suspicion. The law requires that mandated reporters who have reported suspicions to the church also to report those suspicions to the state. The Policy may designate certain people to help mandated reporters. Helpers serving in this support role must never discuss whether to report. Instead, helpers can guide mandated reports on how to report and provide moral support to the reporter.

In some states, the law may not require all adults to report suspicions of child abuse. However, just because a state does not mandate certain adults to report does not mean that they are prohibited from reporting. The law requires the minimum for child safety, but churches can and should go above and beyond the law. Because Jesus calls his church to protect the vulnerable, the Policy should require staff and adult volunteers to report child abuse. The Policy should direct that any member of the church community (regardless of whether they are a mandated reporter) should report abuse they suspect.

How Should a Report Be Filed?

The Policy should direct that a child's disclosure of past or present sexual abuse must be reported to the appropriate state agency in the method the state prescribes (i.e., Child Protective Services or law enforcement) and within the timeframe the state prescribes. To determine the appropriate agency to call for filing a report of known or suspected child abuse in your state, search the Child Welfare Information Gateway.

In general, information pertinent to children is reported to Child Protective Services, and information about a perpetrator is reported to the law enforcement agency (Police Department or Sheriff's Office) within the jurisdiction the abuse allegedly occurred. If a church staff member or volunteer has information about both the

child and the alleged perpetrator, they should report the information to both CPS and to the appropriate law enforcement agency.

The Policy should also mandate public posting of the reporting
phone number alongside fire safety and police phone numbers and
in other public places within the church building.

After a Report Is Filed?

After a report is filed, the child protection agency or law enforcement agency may or may not pursue an investigation or arrest. The
Policy should direct the church to fully cooperate with the investigating authorities.

The Policy can direct any staff members, volunteers, or other
community members to notify church leadership after making a
report. Church leadership should assign a liaison to both the victim
and the alleged offender (more specific instructions are found in
Chapter Thirteen). The church may also need to notify the congregation. The primary purpose of such a notification is to protect
children and to provide an opportunity for other possible victims to
be identified. The timing, method, and content of such a notification should be determined in consultation with the investigating
officer and a GRACE representative or other qualified child protection professional. In these situations, it is critical that the child's
identity be carefully protected, so that the process of responding to
the abuse does not revictimize the child.

The Policy should direct that when a report has been made
and the alleged offender is a staff member or volunteer, the church
should immediately suspend the individual from any church related
activity. No alleged offender should have access to the victim or
any other child. Since any communication to the suspect regarding
the allegations could compromise the criminal investigation, the
timing of this decision should be made in consultation with the

law enforcement officer supervising the investigation and a GRACE Certification Specialist or similar child protection expert.

Your Policy Should Include Information on the Following Reporting Topics

- What information must be reported
- Where to file a report (i.e., child protection agency and/or local law enforcement)
- When to notify the church
- That the church is available to assist in filing reports
- The process for informing the church of concerns regarding child sexual abuse
- What procedures the church will follow upon receiving a report
- A general prohibition against conducting internal investigations
- A commitment to take the necessary investigative and protective actions in cases the child protection agency declines to investigate but the church believes are concerning
- The confidentiality of a report to the church
- The circumstances when and people with whom the confidentiality of a report will be waived
- The circumstances when it is necessary to alert the church community about allegations of abuse, and the manner in which this will be done

---

While reporting may be the right legal and moral action to take, it is a difficult process. In most cases, the church leadership or a community member may have to report someone they know. Reporting abuse is never an easy task. However, having a Policy that provides a reporting protocol makes it easier by helping to ensure that the process is handled the same, regardless of whether the alleged offender is a spiritual leader, colleague, congregant, friend, or family member. It can help to remember that, if the individual has abused a child, then a report is necessary to save the child from further abuse and to protect other children.

A report can also be the first step to bringing an offender to justice. Individuals who abuse children betray the trust of the entire community; they must face the consequences of their criminal actions and not be provided an opportunity to reoffend. For all of these reasons, if you suspect child sexual abuse or other forms of child maltreatment, report the abuse. It is only through our collective resolve to report abuse that we can end child sexual abuse in our community.

Policy Worksheet: Reporting

1. What information does your state require to be reported? Place a check mark by the categories that apply and add any other categories that would fulfill the legal obligation.

» Witnessed abuse
» Children's abuse disclosures
» Consistent and egregious indicators
» A perpetrator's disclosure
» Rumors a child is being abused
»
»
»

2. Who does your state require to report suspected abuse (i.e., mandated reporters)? The church's mandated reporters are:

3. If your state does not designate all adults as mandated reporters, will your Policy ask adults who are not mandated reports to report abuse? _____ yes _____ no

4. Who will the church require to report?

» Pastors
» Staff
» Volunteers
» Church leadership
»
»
»
»

5. How does your state require reports to be made?

6. What is your local sheriff's office number?

7. What is your local child advocacy center's number?

8. If mandated reporters want assistance in making a report, who in church leadership can they contact? Who outside of the church should they contact?

9. After a church member has reported abuse, do you want them to notify someone in church leadership? _____ yes _____ no

10. If yes, what is your internal reporting hierarchy?

> » Example:
> Child > youth volunteer > youth director > senior pastor

11. What is the law and what is your policy regarding abuse disclosed to clergy or staff working in pastoral or other roles (e.g., confession)? Confidentiality/privilege?

12. Will your church include a statement encouraging its members to report abuse?

> **Sample Policy Language:** The abuse of children is not only a sin, but it is a serious crime. When adults report suspected child abuse to the legal authorities, their report could save a child's life. In contrast, silence about suspected abuse brings incredible harm to victims and emboldens offenders. [Faith Church] encourages its members, both mandated reporters and not, to contact the authorities immediately when a child discloses abuse, when they witness child abuse, or when they observe signs of abuse.

CHAPTER ELEVEN

. . . .

INDEPENDENT REVIEWS

Churches should only engage with independent reviews in a very limited number of circumstances. In general, faith communities must leave the investigating to the God-ordained civil authorities who have the requisite training and experience to handle such complex and critically important matters. There are two primary circumstances when a church is recommended to engage in some form of investigation/review.[1]

First, when a suspicion of child maltreatment is reported to the civil authorities and they decline to investigate or prosecute the alleged abuses. There are numerous reasons why the authorities may decide not to move forward with criminal investigations or prosecutions against alleged offenders. Many of those reasons have little or nothing to do with the veracity of the abuse allegations. For example,

- The child is unable to participate in the investigation or testify in court.
- Statute of limitations have expired on the ability to prosecute the crime. In many states, the authorities have only a limited number of years in which to prosecute crimes. For many different reasons, it often takes many years for an abuse survivor to step forward and report the crime.

Unfortunately, sometimes these reports are made after the statute of limitations has expired leaving the authorities with no choice but not to proceed with the case. Yet the statute of limitations has nothing to do with whether the abuse occurred or not.

- Location of alleged abuse. The local authorities are unable to move forward with the case because the offense allegedly occurred in another jurisdiction. For example, a youth pastor may have sexually abused a child while on a missions trip overseas. Local authorities lack jurisdiction to prosecute, and the overseas law enforcement is unable or unwilling to move forward.

- The prosecutor determines that the evidence is insufficient to satisfy the very high burden of proof beyond and to the exclusion of all reasonable doubt. There are so many different reasons that a given prosecutor may decide not to prosecute a child abuse case, including but not limited to, insufficient corroborative evidence.

Second, a prosecuting attorney may not pursue legal prosecution because it is determined that the behavior is not criminal; however, while such behavior might not be criminal, it might still violate the church Policy, be immoral, be inappropriate, or be unsafe. Below are just two examples of the type of behavior that would fall within this category:

- A youth volunteer makes sexually explicit comments regarding a member of the youth group.
- An adult communicates privately online with a child about matters that are inappropriate but not illegal.

In these cases, it may be worth pursuing an independent review. Consult with GRACE or a similar, qualified organization. Experts in child/youth maltreatment will analyze the situation and help determine whether a formal review is an appropriate course of action, or if some other less formal measure would better address the particular situation.[2]

Initiating an Independent Review

An independent review is an objective, third-party investigation to ascertain facts and determine appropriate follow-up steps to assist a church in creating a culture of child protection and regain the trust of abuse victims. Every independent review will look different, given the diversity of organizations and scope of allegations. It is crucial that every independent investigation is 1) completely independent, 2) performed by qualified investigators, and 3) completed by those with specialized experience in the field of child abuse investigation. Even if well-intentioned, a review that lacks any of these three components can have disastrous consequences.

Independent

If it is determined that a formal independent review is needed, whoever conducts the review must first and foremost be independent of your local congregation. If an investigation is conducted by church members, subentities, leaders, or governing bodies, its credibility and legitimacy will understandably be called into question. In legal terms, this is a conflict of interest—those with a stake in the outcome of an investigation should not be performing it. This same principle applies when those conducting the investigation have a personal relationship with the individuals who are witnesses in the investigation. When the safety of children is involved, it is virtually impossible to objectively assess the conduct of a personal friend and to make decisions related to that friend's alleged conduct.

Trained Investigators

Second, because reviews are not a subject taught in seminary and they cannot be learned through watching television shows, churches should hire an organization trained in conducting competent investigations. When unqualified individuals attempt an investigation with the complex, often counterintuitive dynamics of child abuse, victims will suffer. Whether it's interfering with an ongoing law enforcement investigation or simply a lack of training on how to interview witnesses, untrained investigators can do more harm than good. Furthermore, unqualified investigators will miss or misinterpret leads and other information, reaching improper conclusions and doing a further disservice to the very parties that a quality investigation is designed to serve. Lay individuals do not have the training to avoid these and many other pitfalls with devastating personal, spiritual, and legal consequences.

Often, churches believe they may conduct reviews because they have members who are or were law enforcement officers. First, recall the concerns over whether the investigation is actually independent. Second, although law enforcement members are an invaluable addition to the church's culture of child protection, being a police officer does not make you an expert in child abuse investigations or victim dynamics. For example, there is a world of difference in the experience of an officer who mostly writes speeding tickets and the lead detective of a Criminal Investigative Division's Sex Crimes Unit. The traffic control officer has not investigated sex offenses, is unfamiliar with the psychology of sex offenders, does not know effective lines of questioning, and does not know how to effectively probe for previous offenses. Most police officers have very little training and experience in interacting with abuse victims and are simply not equipped to address the needs and vulnerabilities of abused children. The need for an experienced investigator is critical in any investigation related to the alleged abuse of a minor—sexual abuse cases are among the most difficult to investigate and prosecute, and "law enforcement experience" alone does not guarantee that an investigation will meet the high standards that all parties deserve.

In most instances, the organization that oversees the review will be able to conduct the review with a lead investigator.[3] Recognizing that funds will often be very limited, and the importance of expediting the review, it is prudent to have the lead investigator conduct interviews, review documentation, and anything else required to carry out a thorough and objective review. During the course of the review, the lead investigator will be able to consult with the oversight organization to draw upon its expertise as may be necessary.

Expert in Child Maltreatment Dynamics

Just as a person who has heart disease consults with medical professionals specializing in heart disease, churches must also seek assistance from those with significant knowledge and experience in handling cases of child maltreatment. Whoever conducts the review must be experienced in investigating cases of child maltreatment and must have access to current or past law enforcement officers, prosecutors, and mental health and medical experts who are current on the literature pertaining to child abuse and have significant experience in the handling of these cases.[4] Two decades' worth of research documents that most police officers, prosecutors, judges, social workers, law enforcement officers, psychologists, nurses, and physicians are inadequately trained in responding to these complex cases.[5]

Upon completion of each independent review, the investigator will prepare written Factual Findings that will be provided to the oversight organization. Based on the Factual Findings, the oversight organization will make recommendations to the church regarding decisions that should be made regarding the situation.

Policy Worksheet: Independent Investigations

Sample Policy Language:

Under the following circumstances, [Faith Church] will consult with GRACE (or equivalent child protection expert) to determine if an independent review should be pursued:

1. When a suspicion of child maltreatment is reported to the civil authorities and they decline to investigate or prosecute the alleged abuses.
2. A district attorney has not pursued legal prosecution because no suspected criminal behavior is reported; however, the Child Safeguarding Committee believes the individual's behavior might still violate the church policy, be immoral, be inappropriate, or be unsafe.

What circumstances would you add to this list?

What organization would you consult if those circumstances arise?

Sample Policy Language:

If an investigation is deemed necessary, [Faith Church] will retain an organization that meets the following criteria:

1. Completely independent of [Faith Church]
2. Experienced in proper investigation techniques
3. Up-to-date on child maltreatment research

Policy Section Four
Supporting Survivors

When churches learn that a child in its congregation has been abused or an adult member experienced childhood abuse, they can play a vital role in that person's healing. Research has consistently shown that abuse survivors who maintain some connection to their faith experience better mental health outcomes as adults than those who do not.[1] Non-offending, trustworthy clergy can have a particularly powerful role in helping child victims to heal. Whether as a child or adult, survivors often first disclose to a pastor. One child protection expert explains,

> The fact of the matter is that many survivors may actually feel more comfortable disclosing to a trusted spiritual advisor (assuming the perpetrator here is not him or her self a faith leader) than they will to civil authorities at first. Therefore, faith leaders are often placed in the position of a first responder to disclosures of sexual abuse . . . and have an essential and inescapable role to play (in supporting survivors of abuse).[2]

A kind and encouraging clergy member can be a lifeline to a victimized child or adult survivor whose spiritual injuries may require pastoral counseling that a mental health expert is not able to provide. Clergy members are thus increasingly included in multidisciplinary teams that respond to child sexual abuse.[3]

But it is not just clergy who are able to facilitate a survivor's healing. Anyone who provides a survivor with a healthy relationship and support can make a profound difference. What can churches do to help survivors? The following chapters talk specifically about what Policies can help facilitate the support survivors need. Chapter Twelve looks at Policy to support children and adults if they disclose abuse. Chapter Thirteen outlines Policies that can provide long-term support.

CHAPTER TWELVE

. . . .

Abuse Disclosures

Abuse survivors and clinicians tell, in no uncertain terms, that the first step to healing from the trauma of child abuse is to speak about what happened, and that a supportive reception to the disclosure can make all the difference in a survivor's treatment. Yet disclosing abuse can be difficult for survivors because their history of abuse makes trusting another person complicated. One adult survivor relates that she has "had a terrible time with allowing God or anyone else to draw close. It was when I let someone close that they raped me." Although they may not be able to articulate the difficulties so succinctly, children face similar fears and obstacles that make disclosing difficult. The following chapter explores child and adult disclosures, and how your church's Policy can encourage supportive responses.

How Children Disclose

When asked by his parents' friend about how school was going, one eight-year-old responded that school was okay but that there were some very bad kids in his class. When asked what made those kids bad, he described how a few years ago, he found a group of the "bad boys" huddled together behind some bushes during recess. Then the boy stopped, looked up at his parents' friend apprehensively, and

said, "I don't really remember what happened next." Nonchalantly
the friend said, "That's okay. But you should know that if there was
anything you wanted to tell me, you would not get in trouble for
doing so." He said, "Oh, actually I think I remember now. I went
over to the boys and I saw that they all had their pants down and I
could see their, you know . . ." His voice dropped to a whisper. The
eight-year-old continued, "They were all holding down one boy and
touching his privates, and he was crying. And they did something
else, but I don't remember." He looked at his parents' friend, sizing
her up, gauging her reaction to his words so far.

The friend told him that it was good he was sharing this with
her. She repeated how he would not get in trouble for sharing more,
but also any friends he was telling about would not get in trouble
either. Suddenly, this small child remembered the rest of the events,
"Actually, I was the boy they were holding down. I kept begging
them to let me go, but they wouldn't listen!" This adult provided
model responses to the child's disclosure. When developing your
Policy for supporting abuse survivors, it is important to have a basic
understanding of how children disclose, so that you can recognize
a disclosure when it occurs and respond in a similarly supportive
manner.

Older and younger children rarely disclose abuse directly, all at
once, or in a coherent, linear fashion; often they test the waters. If
a child starts disclosing something to you or seems like she wants
to talk, it is your job to listen and help her feel safe. If you suspect
that a child is being abused, maintain ongoing communication with
him so that he has a safe space to disclose the abuse if and when he
is ready.[1] Know that children are often reluctant to disclose abuse.
Most wait years, even decades before telling anyone what happened
to them. If questioned directly, many child victims will deny the
abuse. When children disclose, they almost always do so by accident, and may later recant even when there is proof that the abuse
occurred.[2]

When children disclose intentionally, children may first test the adult's reaction by pretending that the abuse happened to a friend or by supplying only a small bit of information.

- "A kid in my class was making up stories today. He told us that the pastor takes him out for ice cream and licks his penis on the car ride home."
- "Rachel doesn't have to study. The teacher has a crush on her and will let her do extra credit even if she does poorly."
- "I don't like it when Aunt Leah comes over."
- "The boys in the older group are always bothering us before groups start—I hate them!"
- "Pastor Smith is smelly and gross."
- "I want to quit my Bible study."
- "The youth leader beat up a kid at groups this morning. But he deserved it because he wasn't behaving."

If the adult responds emotionally or negatively to the initial statements, the child may stop talking. Given these dynamics, the Policy should direct members how to receive an abuse disclosure from a child. Here are a few suggestions.

Believe the child.

In the moment of a disclosure, your only concern is making sure that you are there to support the child, and this begins by believing. Research tells us that children who are believed when they disclose their abuse develop greater resiliency than those who are not.[3] If a child makes the incredibly difficult decision to disclose abuse, it behooves your church to do everything it can to support the child and protect him and others from future abuse. In summarizing twenty years of work with child abusers, Dr. Anna Salter laments:

In the interviews I have done, they (the perpetrators) have admitted to roughly 10 to 1,250 victims. What was truly frightening was that all the offenders had been reported before by children, and the reports had been ignored.[4]

Love and care for the child.

No matter how anxious, scared, or uncomfortable you are, maintain a calm and caring tone when you speak to the child. All of the questions plaguing you will need to be addressed, but not now. At this moment, the child needs to know that she is loved and protected. Do whatever you can to communicate to the child how much she matters.

Build resiliency.

When children are abused, their abuser steals their agency and controls them to gratify their own wishes. Telling someone about being abused may be the hardest decision a victimized child has ever faced. If a child works up the courage to disclose, look for opportunities to restore some of the power that was taken from him. Rather than saying "you poor child," which reinforces the child's image of himself as a helpless victim, try using words that empower, such as "I'm so glad you came to get help;" "You did the right thing looking for an adult;" "I am very proud of you," or even simply "I'm so glad you told me."

Look for an opening—any opening—to build resiliency by thanking, praising, and reassuring the child that he made the right decision. When an adult listens and affirms the child's courage and goodness, healing begins immediately. Imagine the relief and the personal power for a child who can share with an attentive, engaged adult. Sexually abused children who receive affirmation and psychological help can and do heal.

Don't blame the child.

Under no circumstances should you ever blame the child, even if the child broke a rule or disobeyed you, and this led directly to the abuse. If a child accepted a ride from an adult without checking for permission first, and then was abused by that adult, this is not the time to reprimand the child for breaking her safety rules ("that's why I tell you to always check with me first!"). In these situations, the child is probably already blaming herself. It is your job to reassure her that she is not in trouble, that you are not upset at her, and that the abuse was the adult's fault, and only the adult's fault.

Respond to the child's cues.

Specific language such as, "It is not your fault;" "I believe you;" "You didn't deserve what happened to you" are in general good things to say but may not be appropriate for specific situations. Many children intuit society's reluctance to confront child abuse, or perhaps their abusers have repeatedly blamed them or told them that no one would believe them if they disclosed. These statements are critical messages that should be conveyed; however, it is not always best to state them explicitly. For example, one survivor of childhood sexual abuse recounts the damaging impact of the words "I believe you," spoken by the well-intentioned police officer who took his statement. In that moment, he understood with a crushing clarity, something that until that point had not crossed his mind— that there were those who would not believe him.

Instead, as you listen to the child, listen for indications that the child might be worried about getting in trouble, might be feeling guilty, or might be concerned that you will not believe him. In these instances, do explicitly reassure the child. But absent these indicators, convey these messages in your tone and accepting language instead.

Protect the child.

Your first step after listening to the child will be to figure out what needs to happen to protect this child and other children. If there is an immediate threat to the child's safety, keep the child with you and take action to protect other children. For instance, if a child discloses that her youth group leader abused her and youth groups are currently in session, alert a senior staff member immediately, so that the group leader can be removed from the room. Tell the child that you are going to do everything you can to keep her safe, and that if anything happens that makes her feel unsafe, she should let you know immediately.

Do not offer false reassurances.

Children who have been abused have already had their trust broken, and to the extent possible, we must try not to be another person in their life who betrays them. If a child approaches you and asks you to keep a secret, do not agree, because you may not be able to keep this promise. If the child then clams up, explain that if someone is hurting them or another child, you may need to tell in order to get help. Norman Friedman, an expert child-safety consultant for AMSkier insurance, advises camp counselors to tell the child, "You came to me because you trusted me and you thought I could help you. If that is true, trust me that I will only tell someone if I need to in order to get you help." In Norman's experience, children will then, in most cases, tell you what they wanted to say.

Keep the child informed and involved.

If a child does not begin by asking you to keep a secret, he may end this way, concluding his disclosure with "but you can't tell anyone." Reassure him that you will be as discreet as possible, but that you will need to tell some people because you need to keep him safe. This news can be jarring to a victimized child who already feels like so much is out of his control. Reaffirm for the child that he did the right thing by telling you, and then provide him with as much age-appropriate information and agency as possible. Clearly explain your next steps to the child so that he knows what to expect, and seek his input wherever possible. For instance, if it is unsafe to send the child home and CPS asks you to keep the child at the church, you might ask the child who he wants to wait with him. While the choice to go home is not on the table, the choice for company is. A child's disclosure of abuse, especially familial abuse, sets into motion a whole range of steps that will be out of his hands. Knowing this, wherever it is possible and as it relates to your interactions with him, you want to give the child the power to make decisions about what happens to him.

Be the Adult.

Though you may try your hardest, ultimately the child might be upset at you for needing to tell others what she has told you. The child might get angry or become very afraid. Do not take the child's emotional response personally. Do your best to care for the child, but do not let her resistance prevent you from taking the steps you need to take to protect her. Though she may not realize it now, eventually she may appreciate your help.

Note on Delayed Disclosures

Like children, adults who disclose childhood abuse have had to overcome tremendous internal and external pressures to do so. Unlike children, when adults disclose abuse, their many years of silence may be taken as evidence that the disclosure is untrue. However, delayed disclosure is normal for children who have been abused. The Australian Royal Commission into Institutional Responses to Child Sexual Abuse looked at delays in disclosures among child victims and noted that a number of factors impact the time to disclosure, including age, gender, relationship to the perpetrator, and nature of the sexual abuse. By far though, the longest delays occurred when the perpetrator was in a position of power, responsibility, or authority over the victim, such as a pastor or teacher.[5] Of those cases, the majority of victims kept their silence for at least ten years, often well into adulthood.

Adult Disclosures

When adult victims choose to trust by disclosing their abuse to a pastor, church professional, or lay leader, they have identified that person as someone they can trust to share some of their darkest, most painful memories. Receiving an abuse disclosure is an honor, not a burden; it is a sign of trust. In order to understand more fully how communities can tangibly support survivors of child abuse, we asked them. The following Dos and Don'ts for supporting adults who disclose their childhood abuse were written with feedback from individuals who were abused as children within the Christian community.

Listen.

Listen carefully to the survivor. When receiving an adult abuse disclosure, the best gift people can give survivors is to listen to them, providing them with a calm, non-judgmental, safe place to talk. Allow survivors to set the pace for what and when they disclose.

Survivors will share if and when they choose. Do not pressure them or ask for details.

Believe victims and thank them for their trust.

Many survivors struggle daily with shame and stigma from the abuse. This is especially true of male survivors. Survivors who find the courage to come forward have likely already spent an eternity replaying the abuse and wondering if there was anything they could have done differently. They may have also told themselves a few hundred (perhaps thousand) times that no one is going to believe them if they do disclose. The courage it takes to come forward should be met with nothing short of total and sincere gratitude.[6]

Help victims to feel safe by following their lead.

As the recipient of an abuse disclosure, you may feel many things. In the moment of the disclosure, do your best to stay focused on the survivor and what the survivor needs. Offer assistance in a manner that empowers survivors to be an active participant in their own healing and demonstrates that you will follow their lead. You might do this by asking questions like, "What can I do to help you feel safe right now?" Perhaps the victim would like your support as he discloses to his family. Perhaps she has theological questions related to the abuse that have been plaguing her for years. Perhaps he would like you to tell him that you believe him. Or perhaps she needs nothing more at that moment than a kind presence. The point is that our response in that moment should be determined not by what we want to say, but by what the victims tell us they need.

Never impose forgiveness.

Do not pressure survivors to forgive their abusers. Forcing forgiveness does not allow the wounds of abuse to heal and can retraumatize survivors. One survivor explained how "I felt like such a failure . . . because I was told repeatedly I wasn't forgiving and was remaining bitter when I was processing and trying to heal." When communities respond to an abuse disclosure by pressuring the victim to forgive, the message they send is that the victim is at fault. Victims have already received this false message all too clearly from their abusers. The community can counteract this lie by holding the abuser responsible and creating a safe place for the victim to grieve and heal. First priority for a victim is safety, not forgiveness. One child advocate explains how,

> Far too often I have heard about faith communities forcing survivor and perpetrator into some kind of mediation or reconciliation. This is never an acceptable practice. If a survivor chooses to forgive the person who abused them, that is something that a community can support, perhaps even celebrate if the circumstances are appropriate. But it is never something to be forced upon a victim. To do so is only another form of disempowering and revictimizing that person.[7]

Respect a survivor's boundaries.

Just as survivors forgive at their own pace, they also determine future boundaries for if and how much of their lives they will share with their perpetrator. Survivors should never be forced to attend service, family events, or any other gathering with their perpetrator. Instead, the perpetrator should be asked to leave. If perpetrators are truly repentant, they will understand and respect the survivor's need for safety. As one blogger so articulately said, "Forgiving your abuser does not necessitate letting them back into your life. Forgiving your abuser does not, in any way whatsoever, oblige you to have, or continue having, a relationship with them. Period. Forgiving a snake for biting me doesn't mean I have to again pick up that snake."[8]

Do not impose a timeline for their grief or healing.

Allow survivors to heal on their own timeline and in their own way. The path to healing is a unique path for each survivor, and for those with deep wounds from their trauma, healing may take a lifetime. Healing involves naming and grieving the wounds imposed on the victim as a child; it is a process that may need to happen over and over again. One survivor described,

> Being sexually abused means being wounded at every level of your being. That means that sometimes you will in fact feel healed—which is likely to then bring washing over you great waves of forgiveness and even compassion for your abuser. But later—could be a day, week, or years later—you may find a wave of an altogether different sort pulling you back out to sea, where you will again find yourself cold, lost, and feeling as if you're sinking. That whole back-and-forth dynamic is just part of the healing process. Victims of abuse commonly enough get trapped into believing that because they felt healed and benevolent on Tuesday, there's something wrong with them if on Friday they're back to feeling wounded and bitter. But there's nothing at all wrong or strange about that phenomenon. Again, it's just part of the process.[9]

DO Say[10]	DON'T Say
Thank you for telling me.	Why are you telling me this?
I'm glad you're safe now.	Why didn't you _____ (scream/stop him etc.)?
You did the right thing _____ (asking for help/telling me/reporting the abuse etc.).	What do you mean when you say he abused you? What exactly did he do?
I'm glad you're talking with me.	Tell me more details about what happened.
I'm sorry this happened to you. How can I help?	Why did he do that to you? Had you done something to make him think that was okay?
Take as much time as you need.	You need to forgive and move on.
Things may never be the same, but they can get better.	Don't worry, it's going to be all right.
I am here.	It'll take some time, but you'll get over it.
I stand with you. This congregation stands with you.	Calm down and try to relax.
	Try to be strong.
The following should only be said if the victim indicates these concerns are on his/her mind.	It was so long ago, why are you still letting your abuser win by hanging on to it? Let it go.
It is okay to be angry.	You should get on with your life.
It is okay to still love your abuser.	Time heals all wounds.
It's understandable you're feeling that way.	Out of tragedies good things happen.
Your reaction is not an uncommon response.	You're lucky that _____ didn't happen.
You're not going crazy. These are normal reactions following an assault.	It was God's will. I know how you feel.
I believe you.	Perhaps you misunderstood . . .
It wasn't your fault.	Better to receive punishment in this world than the next.

Policy Worksheet: Abuse Disclosures

Sample Policy Language:

Because children and adult survivors are reluctant to disclose abuse, [Faith Church] acknowledges that survivors who choose to do so need our community's utmost support.

When children disclose, they almost always do so tentatively or by accident, and may later recant even when there is proof that the abuse occurred. If questioned directly, many child victims may deny the abuse. When children disclose intentionally, children may first test the adult's reaction by pretending that the abuse happened to a friend or by supplying only a small bit of information. If a child discloses abuse to you, the following are helpful tips on how to respond in the moment:

- » Stay calm.
- » Show love and respect for the child.
- » Thank the child for telling you and praise the child's courage.
- » If the child expresses guilt or concerns about getting in trouble, reassure the child that no matter what happened he or she is not to blame.
- » If the child expresses concerns about not being believed, reassure the child that you believe him/her.
- » Allow the child to talk freely; do not interrupt, ask the child to repeat words, or probe for details. Use open-ended questions such as "What happened next?" or "Tell me more."
- » Do not offer false assurances, such as promising to keep the child's disclosure a secret.

» Let the child know what to expect next and incorporate their input where possible.

» Protect the child immediately from the suspected offender.

» Report the abuse to authorities and your supervisors/ church leaders.

» Document the disclosure and your report.

» Protect the child's right to privacy and avoid the urge to turn indiscriminately to colleagues, friends, or family for advice. Instead turn to professionals experienced in handling cases of child sexual abuse and to carefully selected individuals who can provide assistance and support to the child and you.

Receiving an adult's abuse disclosure is an honor, not a burden; it is a sign of trust. Victims often choose to disclose their abuse years, even decades, after it occurred. [Faith Church] encourages anyone receiving an adult's abuse disclosure to be guided by the following responses:

DO Say	DON'T Say
Thank you for telling me.	Why are you telling me this?
I'm glad you're safe now.	Why didn't you _____ (scream/stop him etc.)?
You did the right thing _____ (asking for help/telling me/reporting the abuse etc.).	What do you mean when you say he abused you? What exactly did he do?
I'm glad you're talking with me.	Tell me more details about what happened.
I'm sorry this happened to you. How can I help?	Why did he do that to you? Had you done something to make him think that was okay?
Take as much time as you need.	You need to forgive and move on.
Things may never be the same, but they can get better.	Don't worry, it's going to be all right.
I am here.	It'll take some time, but you'll get over it.
I stand with you. This congregation stands with you.	Calm down and try to relax.
	Try to be strong.
The following should only be said if the victim indicates these concerns are on his/her mind.	It was so long ago, why are you still letting your abuser win by hanging on to it? Let it go.
It is okay to be angry.	You should get on with your life.
It is okay to still love your abuser.	Time heals all wounds.
It's understandable you're feeling that way.	Out of tragedies good things happen.
Your reaction is not an uncommon response.	You're lucky that _____ didn't happen.
You're not going crazy. These are normal reactions following an assault.	It was God's will. I know how you feel.
I believe you.	Perhaps you misunderstood . . .
It wasn't your fault.	Better to receive punishment in this world than the next.

CHAPTER THIRTEEN

· · · ·

ONGOING SURVIVOR SUPPORT

In his book on spiritual activism, Rabbi Avi Weiss writes, "the test of spirituality in the synagogue is not how the community receives the most powerful, but how it welcomes the most vulnerable."[1] Christians can heartily agree as they follow Jesus's admonition to "let the little children come to me and do not hinder them, for to such belongs the kingdom of heaven" (Matthew 19:14). Certainly among the most vulnerable people in the church are those whose innocence was trampled early on by adults in their lives. Beyond responding compassionately to disclosures of abuse, there are concrete steps your church can take to create a supportive environment for those who have experienced childhood abuse. Especially if the alleged offender is a member of the church's congregation, the days and weeks following an abuse disclosure can feel chaotic and confusing. Planning ongoing survivor support before churches find themselves in that situation brings clarity and guidance to difficult circumstances. There are many ways a Policy can outline ways the church will support survivors in a consistent manner. Below are a few suggestions.[2]

Public Support

One of the most basic ways to support a victim is to simply show up. If and when a case goes to trial, church leaders and community members can fill the benches in support of the victim. When a case is not in court, but otherwise becomes known throughout the community, the pastor and congregation should similarly support the victim. This is especially true when the abuser is a respected member of the congregation and the child is being discredited or otherwise disparaged. If the abuse in question happened in your church or by a representative of your church, make sure to stand up for the victim and offer unequivocal public and private apologies.

If both the alleged perpetrator and victim are members of the church, no victim should have to attend church with their alleged perpetrator. Immediately suspend or terminate the alleged perpetrator from any church positions he or she may hold, pending the results of an investigation. The church may assign a liaison to maintain contact with the alleged perpetrator. This type of situation may also call for implementing a Limited Access Agreement. Ultimately, when considering how to handle an alleged perpetrator who attends the same church as the victim, the Policy should encourage the church to reach out to the GRACE Certification Specialist or a similar expert for guidance.

There will be instances where you feel torn in supporting the victim, because the accused is also a member of your congregation, or, for other reasons, you find yourself believing the defendant and not the child. A measured response is wise as it relates to supporting due process. Churches may decide to address the alleged perpetrator's spiritual needs that do not jeopardize the safety of children (e.g., pastoral counseling). Yet the primary focus of the church must be supporting and ministering to the child and his/her family. The policy needs to articulate this focus as it outlines a protocol for how the church will demonstrate such support.

Keep in mind, other victims and perpetrators will most likely be watching from the sidelines, and what they see from their spiritual leaders and congregation tells them much about the consequences they would face for their own case. The manner in which the church responds to an abuse disclosure can either encourage victims to speak or silence them. It can either embolden unknown offenders to continue abusing or drive them to a less vigilant environment. In one instance, a prominent member of a Christian community publicly disclosed his childhood sexual abuse by a pastor. The backlash that followed his disclosure was swift and immediate: his intentions were impugned and his family was ostracized from the community. When asked why they did not stand up for the victim, other pastors in the community justified their inaction by explaining that they had really wanted to support the victim, but as no other victims came forward, they were *forced* to conclude that the pastor had been falsely accused and decided to support him instead. In fact, at least four other victims came forward privately to mental health professionals in the community. But after seeing the community's response to the first victim, who himself was a respected spiritual leader, they felt certain that their own disclosures would never be believed and chose to remain silent.

The Policy should commit to protecting the privacy of all victims of child abuse. All too often child victims of abuse are publicly marginalized while communities rally to protect abusers. In the event that a victim of abuse is publicly attacked or disparaged for the abuse or their response to the abuse, the church leadership should—in consultation with the victim and the victim's family—make a public statement denouncing and prohibiting such treatment of the victim and urge the community to offer support instead. If the disparagement occurs privately, the church leadership will communicate the same message privately to the relevant individuals.

One of the best ways to show this support is to assign a member of the church's leadership to help the family and to express the church's unequivocal support. This person will be designated as a "Support Person(s)."[3] Understanding that abuse can have ongoing impact on a child and a child's family, the Support Person can seek permission from the child and the child's family to continue offering support on an ongoing basis. This support may include:

- Showing up
- Listening
- Affirming
- Offering to accompany the child/family in filing a police report, meeting with Child Protective Services, to court hearings or trial and other related meetings, interviews, or hearings
- Asking the child and the child's family how else the church can offer support

Support People must be careful to avoid causing further harm, and under no circumstances—even when the abuse is alleged and not proven—will they:

- place any portion of blame for the abuse on the child or the child's family
- probe for intimate details of the abuse
- express disbelief of the child
- attempt to silence the child or the child's family in any way or for any reason
- encourage noncompliance with the law
- express support of the perpetrator
- urge reconciliation with or forgiveness of the perpetrator

Therapeutic support

Abuse is not something a child just gets over. If a child's family or adult survivor cannot access such services on their own, the Policy should direct your church to assist them in finding the right therapist, and the right subsidies if necessary. When a child is abused at the church, at a church program, or by a church employee or volunteer, the Policy should outline what steps the church will take to assist the child's family in finding qualified treatment. It is encouraged that the Policy direct the church to pay the cost of therapy at a therapist of the family's choosing. Some churches will offer to provide the child with therapeutic services from someone selected or approved by the church. Such an approach is not focused on the child, but upon the church's desire to direct and control the healing process. It is imperative that a victim's healing is not dictated by the very church responsible for the abuse.

A qualified treatment provider should be a licensed counselor/ therapist with specific training and experience in working with survivors of trauma—child abuse and sexual assault. While clergy may be very qualified to counsel in many areas, most do not have the training and expertise to adequately help those who have been traumatized and may cause further damage.

Pastoral support

One advocate writes of a victim who searched for a "new church home with a pastor who was sensitive to her pain, was willing to walk through dark valleys with her, and was willing to coordinate his spiritual counseling with the work of her medical and mental health providers. Without this pastor, the woman told me, she would have died."[4] Another victim came to her pastors because while she was repeatedly sexually abused, her offender hummed a certain hymn. As a woman, she wanted to go to church but was scared she would hear the same hymn, be reminded of the abuse, and lose control of her emotions in front of the congregation. In hearing this, the pastor promised not to play the hymn during services. Pastors and church leaders who display this sort of kindness are best suited to meet the spiritual needs of survivors.[5]

Child abuse experts recommend that therapists who treat victims of abuse work together with pastors as a team to address both the victim's emotional and spiritual recovery.[6] Pastors might find themselves overwhelmed in this role, unsure of where the line between pastoral counselor and mental health professional lies, or how to know the difference between a spiritual question and one that reflects deeper underlying mental health issues. It is good to note this tension and to discuss it upfront with the victim's therapist. Make sure that you work together with the therapist, and that you can turn to the therapist for guidance when you need it. No matter how well-intentioned, do not delve beyond your area of expertise.

Sometimes the victim has deep theological questions. Many times, it is not the pastor's answer to these questions that is so important, but rather that the questions are allowed to be asked; that the pastor creates a safe space where the victim is permitted to express anger at God, walk through turbulent situations, and feel the hard emotions. When pastors treat the victims in a way that affirms their value as a precious human being made in the image of God, they can experience healing. Furthermore, pastors can refute many theological errors and lies abusers use.

Community support

There are also several communal actions churches can take to help survivors heal. All the support given to victims on a personal basis can be given within the community as well. The Policy should encourage your church to speak about abuse often, give sermons, and offer trainings about abuse dynamics and how to respond well. Consider giving public prayers for healing, justice, and support for abuse victims. When giving public talks about child abuse, also give advance notice to the congregation. This way parents can choose whether or not they wish their children to be present, and adults with their own histories of child abuse, who may be triggered by the content, can prepare in advance, bring a support person, or choose not to attend.

If abuse occurred within your church community, victims want the assurance there will never be a minimization or revisionist history. Communities support victims by telling the truth about abuse. When we forget or refuse to acknowledge what happened, sadly, history is often repeated. Some communities have even chosen to build a memorial or plant a garden for abuse that has occurred within their community as a way of marking the past.

Policy Worksheet: Ongoing Survivor Support

Sample Policy Language: The purpose of this Policy is to prevent occurrences of child abuse. Yet we understand that no matter how hard we try to protect children, there will always be some individuals seeking to harm them. If [Faith Church] becomes aware that a child has been, or is suspected to have been, abused, they will take the following steps to clearly communicate support for the child and the child's family:[7]

Terminate/Suspend. Immediately suspend or terminate the alleged perpetrator of abuse from any church positions s/he may hold, pending the results of an investigation. Assign a liaison to maintain contact with the alleged perpetrator.

Support Person. A member of the church's leadership will be designated as a "Support Person(s)" and will reach out to the child and the child's family[8] within twenty-four hours of learning of the abuse to express the church's unequivocal support. Understanding that abuse can have ongoing impact on a child and a child's family, the Support Person will seek permission from the child and the child's family to continue offering support on an ongoing basis. This support will include:

» Showing up
» Listening
» Affirming
» Offering to accompany the child/family in filing a police report, meeting with Child Protective Services, to court hearings or trial and other related meetings, interviews, or hearings

» Asking the child and the child's family how else the church can offer support

Support People will understand the limitations of their role and will not offer therapeutic, legal, or other expert advice, but will instead function as members of a multidisciplinary team, working when possible to support and complement the efforts of involved professionals to support the child and family. For instance, a child who has been abused may have theological questions or experience spiritual injuries, but at the same time, may find comfort in spirituality, prayer, and other forms of religious engagement. The pastor has a unique role to fill here and will make himself/herself available to provide regular ongoing pastoral support to the child and the child's family.

Support People will be careful to avoid causing further harm, and under no circumstances—even when the abuse is alleged and not proven—will Support Individuals:

» place any portion of blame for the abuse on the child or the child's family
» probe for intimate details of the abuse
» express disbelief of the child
» attempt to silence the child or the child's family in any way or for any reason
» encourage noncompliance with the law
» express support of the perpetrator
» urge reconciliation with or forgiveness of the perpetrator

Mental Health Treatment. The church will offer to help the family find a qualified mental health practitioner with expertise treating victims of abuse and their family members. If the family requires assistance paying for mental health treatment, the church will offer to subsidize such treatment or connect the family to resources that may be able to assist in this regard. In the event that the child is found to have been abused by a church employee, volunteer, or other individual serving in an official capacity, or that the church was negligent or otherwise complicit in allowing the abuse to happen, the church will reimburse the entire cost of treatment for the child and the child's family members.

Public Support. The church commits to protecting the privacy of all victims of child abuse. We also understand that all too often child victims of abuse are publicly marginalized while communities rally to protect abusers. In the event that a victim of abuse is publicly attacked or disparaged for the abuse or their response to the abuse, the church leadership will—with the victim's permission— make a public statement denouncing and prohibiting such treatment of the victim and urge the community to offer support instead. If the disparagement occurs privately, the church leadership will communicate the same message privately to the relevant individuals.

Creating a Culture of Ongoing Support for Victims of Childhood Abuse. Our church aims to create a space that is safe for all victims of childhood abuse—both those we know about and those we don't. To this end, the church will:

» Create and distribute a referral list of local organizations and therapists who specialize in sexual abuse prevention and treatment
» Post signs throughout the church building about child abuse prevention and reporting
» Host a support group for adults who have experienced childhood abuse
» Publicize the Policy, communicating that this institution takes child protection seriously and does not tolerate abuse
» Speak about child abuse publicly and often

   - Annual sermons by the pastor on this topic

- ~ Initiate communal dialogue
- ~ Post the contact information for church leaders who are available to answer any questions about child safety

Highlight the sample Policy language you will include in your church's Policy. What would you add?

Policy Section Five
Living the Policy

The purpose of formalizing your Policy in writing is so that your church can live it. The Policy's goals are to create a safer environment for children, make violations socially unacceptable and immediately recognizable, allow adults to intervene at early indicators of abuse, and keep your community up-to-date with best practices in the child protection field. Your church has invested much time and effort in developing a comprehensive Policy, but if the Policy remains on the back shelf, it will not protect children. For your Policy to achieve its goals, churches must clearly communicate it to members, educating them about the terms of the Policy and child abuse dynamics. The community must know and live the Policy.

The Policy's terms may require community members to embrace new habits. Before expecting shifts in behavior though, churches must make sure that community members are educated, so that they can understand why they are being asked to think and act in new ways. When staff, volunteers, and parents understand the Policy and the reasons for it, they are empowered to abide by its provisions and children are more protected. Helping the community understand the reasons for the protective practices goes a long way in generating the support necessary for your Policy to be effective in creating a culture of child safety that pervades every aspect of your church.

Your church should sponsor training as it unveils the Policy for the first time and as part of its ongoing effort to protect children.

Educating every member of the community, including children, parents, staff, congregants, and visitors helps create a culture of child-protection where adults are equipped with the tools necessary to give children their best chance at a most basic right—a childhood free from maltreatment. A good Policy also adheres to best practices in child protection. Keeping the Policy up-to-date with the reality in your church and with emerging research requires ongoing revisions and updates. This is the essence of a living, breathing document—regular maintenance of your Policy keeps it strong. Chapter Fourteen explores how to reveal your Policy for the first time and create ongoing trainings for your church. Chapter Fifteen discusses how to update and revise your Policy.

CHAPTER FOURTEEN

. . . .

TRAINING AND DISSEMINATION

Before church members can abide by the Policy, they must know about and understand it. When churches receive regular child abuse prevention and response training from qualified individuals, they are empowered to abide by the Policy and protect the church's children. Individuals who have not thought much about how to keep children safe may be unaware of the risks present in a church and resistant to change. Others who have thought about the issue, but never received any formal training may not understand the necessity of the new protocols. A series of trainings for the entire community along with a pastor's sermon introducing the topic will go far in minimizing resistance to the Policy.

As the community begins to understand the gravity of the issue and its prevalence, they will also want to know what is being done to protect children in their own church. This is a good opportunity to show how the Policy keeps children safe. In this way, Policy dissemination and training go hand-in-hand. The GRACE Certification process provides the training and helps with Policy dissemination for participating churches.

Training and Dissemination Are Necessary to Accomplish the Policy's Goals

Policy Goals

Goal 1: The Policy will create a safer environment for children in the church.

Goal 2: Policy violations will be socially unacceptable and immediately recognizable.

Goal 3: Policy violations will serve as early indicators of potential abuse.

Goal 4: Adults can report suspected abuse as necessary.

Goal 5: The Policy will be a living, breathing document that is frequently updated to reflect best practices in the field of child protection.

To achieve these goals, the Policy must be clearly communicated and easily accessible so that

Goal 1: Staff and congregants know and live its terms.

Goal 2: Staff and congregants become intimately familiar with its terms and able to recognize violations.

Goal 3: Violators will have known of the Policy's terms and be unable to claim ignorance as a defense.

Goal 4: Adults who report will know that the church leadership supports them.

Goal 5: Churches can receive feedback from the congregation about unclear or problematic terms.

Policy Dissemination

Your Policy should be disseminated as widely as possible via multiple channels. The precise communication mechanisms you choose will partly depend upon those already in place in your church and may include: posting the Policy on your church's website, placing a stack of hard copies in your lobby or main office, talking about the Policy regularly from your pulpit, sending a semiannual email to your membership with a link to the Policy, highlighting a Policy term in your church's monthly newsletter, creating a poster of the Policy's main points to hang in the youth center, and including a copy of the Policy in new-member packets.

For instance, one church includes a note on the bottom of every flier indicating that their church is wheelchair accessible, and that anyone requiring additional accommodations should reach out to the programming director. In this small way they are sending a continuous and clear message of inclusion that begins to permeate every aspect of their program. You want to help your church do the same thing with child protection.

The terms of the Policy should also be informally communicated on a regular basis. This is especially important when the Policy is first released and the congregation is still trying to digest the new terms and figure out how they apply on the ground. In these first few months, the relevant parts of the Policy should be stated at the beginning of each program along with an explanation of how these terms help to keep children safe. With time, these rules will become standard operating procedure, but are still worth formally reviewing with participants on a periodic basis. If congregants or staff struggle to adjust to the new Policy, they should be gently reminded of its existence and redirected. As congregants become accustomed to the Policy, it may be unnecessary to repeat the terms at the start of each program; instead, individual rules should be stated and accompanied by a simple explanation as they come up in daily functioning. By speaking about child protection often and without making a big deal of it, it will become just another thing that your congregation thinks about before planning or acting. This will help shift the culture of the church.

For employees and regular volunteers, the Policy should be a central component of orientation meetings and ongoing service. As discussed in screening procedures, new volunteers and staff should receive the Policy and discuss its terms during their interviews. Youth directors should include reminders of Policy terms frequently to their youth leaders, parents, and youth participants, going over pertinent Policy terms as they prepare for particular events. For example, before a weekend retreat, the youth director should review the Policy regarding sleeping arrangements, adult-child ratios, transportation, and safe, nurturing touch. Before a week of Vacation Bible School, a children's ministry director should review safety rules pertinent to the week's activities.

In addition to receiving a copy of the Policy, all employees and volunteers should be required to sign an affirmation indicating that they understand its terms and are willing to abide by its terms. Churches may also wish to require signed affirmations from their congregants as a condition of participation in church services and programs or as a requirement for membership. All affirmations should be kept on file in the church office, as proof that the individual or group was informed of the Policy and agreed to its terms.

All of these procedures for disseminating the Policy and securing commitments to abide by it help to protect children. A church in which employees and congregants are intimately familiar with the Policy is a church in which Policy violations will be socially unacceptable and immediately recognizable.

Training

The main focus of any training will be to educate about the terms of the Policy and how to prevent, detect, and respond to child abuse. It can be theoretical and emphasize understanding grooming behavior and why children are reluctant to disclose abuse. It should also be practical and emphasize how to safely take a child to the bathroom or what to do if a child goes missing. GRACE trains churches, and many child advocacy centers are also able to provide general training on child abuse and prevention best-practices.

> *Suggested Content for Staff and Volunteer Training*
>
> - Review the terms of the Policy with all staff and volunteers.
> - Provide additional intensive training for those who work directly with children. Topics might include:
>   - Prevention: practical training on how to implement the Policy and on bystander intervention
>   - Detection: spotting risky behaviors in adults and physical, behavioral, and emotional indicators in children
>   - Response: supporting survivors and reporting externally and internally
> - Coordinate special training for young children and teens on body safety and empowerment skills

We recommend that youth-serving institutions retrain their staff and employees every year. In addition, the best trainings are not one-off events, but incorporated into an ongoing educational plan for the churches. Churches should include guidelines for the frequency of staff and volunteer training and retraining.

As churches regularly conduct trainings and sermons on child protection, more of their congregants will be exposed to child protection principles, and everyone who comes through the doors of the church will receive training of some kind in child protection. For those in a position of responsibility over youth, the training should be the most comprehensive, but all church employees—even those who do not work directly with children—should at least receive a basic training so that they can abide by the Policy. Non-employee individuals who interact with children (e.g., volunteers and parents) need training so that they understand what steps to take and what to look out for in keeping their children safe.

Though much of the parenting role occurs outside the church, when churches offer training for parents, they lead the way for community-wide child protection efforts and help to keep children safe both in and out of the church. Also, consider age-specific educational classes for children. GRACE incorporates a safety skills class for elementary school children and one for teenagers in its Certification, and child advocacy centers often offer classes. Appendix Three also offers a discussion of how to train children in an age-appropriate way.

Policy Worksheet: Education and Dissemination

Activity: Setting Your Policy Up for a Successful Unveil

1. What formal training will accompany the initial dissemination of your Policy? _____

_____

_____

2. Beyond formal training, how else will you raise awareness about child protection and communicate your Policy? *Below, circle the suggestions that are achievable in your church, cross out those that are not, and add your own ideas to the empty lines:*

» Post your Policy on the church's website
» Keep a stack of printed Policies in the lobby, main office, or children's wing
» Send an email to your membership with a link to the Policy (Frequency _____)
» Summarize your Policy in the church's newsletter (Frequency _____)
» Include a copy of your Policy in new-member packets
» Talk about your Policy regularly from the pulpit (Frequency_____)
» Lecture from a child protection expert
» Talk from an adult congregant who has experienced childhood abuse
» Hold a congregational meeting, or multiple smaller meetings, where the church presents the Policy's terms
» As part of your regular training, educate employees, volunteers, and congregants on the contents of the Policy and how to abide by its terms

» _____

» _____

3. In the church, which community members will you reach out to help generate buy-in for the Policy? What will their role be?

Key Board Members: _____

Key Staff Members: _____

Key Volunteers: _____

Key Congregants: _____

Sample Policy Language: Dissemination

> This Policy shall be disseminated widely to the church community through publications, public discussion, educational opportunities, sermons, training programs, and other appropriate means of communication that will raise awareness and create a safe environment for our children. Specifically, the most current version of our Policy shall be
>
> » posted on the church website
> » readily available in the church office, lobby, and nursery
> » communicated to every member semi-annually via email
> » included in new-member packets
> » summarized and posted on the wall in the youth wing
> » incorporated into a sermon delivered annually by the senior pastor

Strike through the bullet points that will not work in your church.

What would you add to help disseminate your church's Policy?

Training Chart: Fill in the following with people in your church who may need to attend training. What type of training will be required? Will the training be required? How frequent will it be (annual, semiannual, quarterly, monthly)?

Group	Type?	Mandatory?	Frequency?
Church staff			
Parents			
Congregants			
Visitors			
Church volunteers			
Church leadership			
Younger children			
Teens			

Who in your church will be required to sign an affirmation indicating that they have read, understand, and commit to abide by the terms of the Policy? When will they be required (e.g., when they begin working with children? Annually?)?

Individuals	Required?	When?
Employees		
Volunteers		
Contractors		
Subcontractors		
Members		
Non-member congregants		
Program participants		
Lessees or others who use space in the church		

Sample Policy Language:

The church requires all staff, volunteers working with children, parents, and church leaders to sign an affirmation indicating that they have read and agree to abide by the terms of this Policy, as a precondition to engagement with the church or receiving access to children. Affirmations will be stored in the church's office files.

CHAPTER FIFTEEN

. . . .

Evaluating and Updating the Policy

After churches develop their Policy, train their congregation members, and implement the Policy, they may encounter difficulties as their community lives out the terms. Language that seemed crystal clear during the Policy development stage may actually be ambiguous in practice; well-intentioned new guidelines may introduce their own unanticipated risks; certain standards may simply be too onerous to follow in a given church. This can feel discouraging and overwhelming. Remember that no Policy is perfect. In fact, regularly reviewing the Policy, listening to feedback, and revising it makes the Policy stronger. Having a Policy that is tailored to your church's context and embraced by the community creates a culture of protection that is far stronger than any one term of a Policy. Regularly evaluating and updating the Policy is necessary to ensure that the language of the Policy reflects the reality on the ground in your church. To evaluate and update its Policy, churches should meet regularly to discuss:

a. Concerning incidents and Policy violations
b. Feedback from parents and children
c. Staff evaluations

    d. The community list of individuals who have Limited Access Agreements

    e. An expert evaluation of the Policy

The frequency of the evaluations may change over time, as churches may want to meet more often following the Policy's roll-out but less often as the Policy becomes standard operating procedure. Whatever frequency churches choose for evaluation meetings, these terms should be expressly included in the Policy. If they are not, the review process runs the risk of being overshadowed by the more pressing needs of daily operation and neglected indefinitely.

Summary of Incident Reports

As discussed in Chapter Eight: Policy Violations and Chapter Ten: Reporting, whenever an individual violates the Policy or someone in the church reports abuse, churches may choose to document those times in an Incident Report. All Incident Reports received during a particular evaluation period should be reviewed as part of the evaluation process and summarized for inclusion in the general membership report. The summary should include the quantity and nature of these reports as well as any follow-up measures taken. See Appendix Two for a sample Incident Report and for a sample form to use in summarizing them.

Feedback from Parents, Children, and Staff

Parents, children, and staff hold information that is critical for the church's review process. In developing a Policy, including a formal mechanism for soliciting feedback from them will yield invaluable information for the church and empower parents and staff to take part in creating a culture of safety. A targeted questionnaire may prompt discussion about the Policy that yields constructive feedback that can improve the Policy. Furthermore, individuals who may have been reluctant to fill out an Incident Report may be more willing to complete an anonymous form they view as part of standard church procedure being filled out by all families. Sample forms are included in Appendix Two.

Review of Limited Access Agreements

Churches should review their list of Limited Access Agreements on a regular basis. For each individual with an Agreement, churches should complete the form found in Appendix Two. If in the process of completing this form, unmanaged risks or other neglected areas are identified, churches should devise a plan and timeline for addressing these risks as soon as possible.

Expert Review

Research and best field practices in child protection are constantly evolving; what may have been cutting edge when your church first develops its Policy can quickly become outdated. In addition, whenever churches revise the Policy, they may unknowingly introduce new risks. As such, it is essential that the Policy be reviewed by an expert in the field of child protection. If your church participates in GRACE's Certification, your Certification Specialist will review your Policy on the following occasions:

- Before it is introduced for the first time
- Whenever a revision is made
- On a regular basis regardless of whether it has been revised since its last expert review

After the expert reviews the Policy and approves its terms, the revisions can be finalized. At this point, churches should add the date of the most recent revision to the beginning or end of the Policy, and also include the date when the next review is due. Churches should make sure that the congregation receives an updated version of the Policy whenever it is revised or ratified, and that all distributed copies of the Policy—whether hardcopy (e.g., in the church office) or digital (e.g., on the church website)—are updated to include the most recent revisions.

Policy Worksheet: Revising and Updating the Policy

How often will feedback about the Policy be solicited?

Which groups of people will be asked for their feedback?

What forms need to be reviewed regularly at your church?

Who will oversee this process?

Who will review the feedback?

Try filling in the following:

Review	How often?	By whom?	Presented to whom?
Incident Reports			
Parental Feedback			
Staff Feedback			
Children's Feedback			
Limited Access Agreements			
Expert Review			

Sample Policy Language:

The following language will be included at the end of [Faith Church's] Policy.

This policy is adopted by action of the _____

_____

this _____ day of _____ .

This Policy was last reviewed by:

[Child Safeguarding Committee Members]:_____

_____

_____

on _____ .

Outside Expert Reviewer: _____

on _____ .

CONCLUSION

. . . .

A Word of Encouragement

Developing, implementing, and updating a Policy is a lot of work for a congregation to undertake, but it's effort well spent. The Policy, far more than a piece of paper, is a tangible expression of love toward your church's children and adult survivors of child abuse. As the apostle John exhorts Christians, love is our identifying mark, "Beloved, let us love one another, for love is from God, and whoever loves has been born of God and knows God" (1 John 4:7). Think of the child who is experiencing abuse and who does not know that God is "the helper of the fatherless" (Psalm 10:14b). Through the Policy, your church is now equipped to intervene and show God's love to this child. Imagine the adult survivors who have "no one to comfort them" (Ecclesiastes 4:1b). Your Policy now guides your church how to bring comfort and tangible support. The team at GRACE is thankful your church is on this journey of protecting children in its care. Let us know if we can assist you along the way.

APPENDIX ONE

. . . .

FORMING A COMMITTEE

Churches should begin their efforts to prevent and respond to child sexual abuse by forming a standing Child Safeguarding Committee (Committee). The Committee will develop, implement, and maintain a comprehensive a Child Protection Policy (Policy). This appendix will help guide you as you define the Committee's roles, select its members, and take preliminary steps to set them up for success.

The Committee's Role

The Committee bears two weighty tasks: limiting opportunities for child abuse and responding to allegations of abuse. To complete these tasks, the Committee's work will include two phases:

Phase I: Front work

1) *Policy Development:* creating a Policy that will provide clear protocols to guide staff and congregants in preventing and responding to child abuse.
2) *Education and Implementation:* communicating the Policy's terms to the entire congregation and developing mechanisms to implement it properly.

Phase II: Ongoing work

3) *Ongoing Evaluation and Maintenance:* meeting regularly as a standing committee in order to evaluate the church's compliance with the Policy and consider revisions to the Policy as necessary.

4) *Advisement:* answering questions about the Policy and advising on child safety issues.

5) *Compliance and Response:* responding to policy violations and other allegations of misconduct or abuse quickly and skillfully.

The Committee's ongoing role means that there will be a continuous presence at the church of individuals who are trained in child-safety. Much of the training your Committee receives will happen naturally as they make their way through this workbook. Additional training will come from experts in the field, such as GRACE's Certification Specialists, who will advise them as they work to develop and execute a comprehensive child protection plan. The knowledge the Committee acquires will help them guide the church in preventing opportunities for abuse, and just as importantly, to know when a situation requires consultation with an outside expert on child safety.

The Committee's Formation

Selecting the right members will set your Committee up for success. Take the time up front to determine the right number of Committee members and consider the characteristics of helpful members, as this will make your Committee stronger and their task easier. Members who have expertise to contribute are good candidates, but laypeople without expertise can be just as valuable if they have a desire to learn, time to devote, and the character to work well with others. Just as the Committee's top priority is to keep children safe, so must its members prioritize safety.

Committee Size

When considering the Committee's size, avoid extremes. Invite enough members to include individuals representing a variety of concerns, but keep the Committee small enough to be discreet and efficient. In one church, the board recruited the very best of their Ivy-educated congregation to be on the Committee—eighteen members. Unfortunately, so many passionate voices at the table hindered progress on even the minutest detail. After six months, the Committee only managed to negotiate one topic in their Policy. The Committee's large size led to unnecessary frustration and division. Conversely, a small Committee means a heavy workload for its members, and such a big demand on people's time can lead to burnout. A Committee of four to five people tends to be ideal for efficiency and still contains sufficient voices for healthy discussion. Even so, it might be wise to begin with a group of eight people, as Committees tend to dwindle in size over time.

Consider your church. What number makes sense for your context?

Expertise

The ideal Committee includes a variety of voices who have expertise relevant to developing the Policy. This expertise may include professional experience in child protection, working or volunteering in the church, or parental experience raising a child in the church. Consider extending invitations to church members who are:

- experts in child protection such as a child abuse prosecutor, a victim's advocate, or a mental health professional who treats abuse victims or sex offenders;

- parents who can remain calm and productive in the face of difficult conversations;
- church professionals who are familiar with the practical realities of the pastoral, youth, and administrative staff;
- lay leaders who carry the responsibility of ensuring a safe church;
- lawyers who can advise the Committee on state and local laws; or
- professionals experienced with drafting policies or ensuring policy compliance (e.g., human resources or corporate managers);
- Survivors of child sexual abuse who have received substantive and professional care and counsel who can contribute a much-needed voice to the committee.

When extending an invitation to a survivor, do so with care and confidentiality. When asking survivors to serve, allow them decide how much of their personal histories they will share with the Committee and empower them to choose a role where they feel safe to give their insights.

Character

Beyond expertise, consider a potential member's character. Committee members should be emotionally stable, capable of having difficult conversations in a respectful manner, and generally cooperative. These character traits go a long way in making a challenging task significantly easier. Anyone who struggles to speak civilly, is consumed with a tangential agenda, or fosters an unhealthy interaction dynamic should not be invited onto the Committee. In order for the Committee to function properly, its members must be able to work together. No matter how intelligent or what level of expertise, if a Committee member is belligerent, verbally abusive, or dismissive of other Committee members, it will be hard for the Committee to make progress.

Experiencing conflict on the Committee is not unheard of given the sensitive nature of the work and members' unique personal histories. If certain Committee members have an interaction-style that impedes progress or they seem fixated on counter-productive agendas, the Committee chair might check with them in an effort to refocus the dialogue and foster more collaboration. When possible, the goal is to continue working together, since diversity of opinion, different operating styles, and pushback can be helpful in developing a nuanced Policy. If a private conversation is ineffective at resolving the problem, the Committee may wish to consult with a trained community mediator to help resolve the conflict. An experienced mediator can help the group work through various difficulties, and often in just one or two sessions, get the Committee back on track. However, even the best efforts to resolve conflict can fail. In the event that the Committee cannot move forward with the problematic individuals, relieve those Committee members of their duties or find a new role for them off of the main Committee.

Before finalizing the Committee's composition, churches should properly screen each candidate. The Committee will be unable to properly protect if one of its members abuses children or enables abusers. Beyond these basic screening measures, the church should ensure that Committee members' goals and expectations align with the Committee's goals and expectations: to protect children. One simple question to ask potential members is why they want to be on the Committee. If, during the selection process, you feel that an individual may not share the same goals, trust that instinct and find another person.

Before Drafting a Policy

Talking about child abuse can be distressing, and a portion of the Committee may have personal histories related to abuse, making the topic even more distressing. Before beginning Policy discussions, the Committee can take preliminary steps to care for its members. Set aside time to learn about each other and to learn together about the dynamics of child abuse and the process of Policy development.

Education about CSA

The Committee must gain a foundational understanding of child abuse if they are to write an effective Policy. In GRACE's Child Safeguarding Certification, Committee members have reading and educational goals to complete with support on how to achieve those goals. If you are not participating in the certification, numerous websites, including many state government sites, offer short, online trainings.

Committees may also want to consult with outside experts such as child advocacy centers, local law enforcement agencies, district attorney offices, or social service departments. GRACE developed this workbook in conjunction with its Child Safeguarding Certification because working with a professional in the field yields tremendous benefits to the Committee as it develops policy for or responds to abuse allegations within the church.

Education about the process

Educating the Committee and setting guidelines about the process as it forms will help the Committee avoid problems or overcome problems later in the process. Take time before addressing Policy matters to establish expectations about tone and Committee by-laws. A sample can be found at the end of this appendix.

Inform the Committee that the tone of discussions will include open dialogue, supportive listening, and respectful disagreement. To accomplish this goal, the Committee might wish to establish customs to help remind them of their mission at the start of each meeting. An example of such a custom might be to read a short excerpt from a victim's writings or to establish a prayer asking God to guide the Committee's work in developing the Policy.

The Committee should be mindful to avoid alarmist tones and to respect the privacy and dignity of their congregants. Abuse of a child is a scary thing to consider, and conversations about abuse prevention can quickly take on an urgent tone, with each word the Committee drafts for their Policy feeling like a matter of life or death. These feelings come from a natural and good place—valuing the seriousness and the importance of the language used. But with so much depending on each word, the Committee can also feel paralyzed. Before the Committee starts work, acknowledge this emotion. If your Committee finds itself paralyzed, try to focus on accomplishing a small goal: finishing one section of one chapter. Remind the Committee that their work does not need to be perfect. The Committee will seek feedback from experts before publishing the Policy, and once published the Policy will be revised and updated on a regular basis.

In addition to addressing tone, take time for the Committee to determine a process for working together. Determining process in advance can help anchor the Committee as it works through difficult topics and can also protect the Committee should anyone question the procedures that were followed in developing the Policy. Below are some topics to consider when drafting bylaws:

- Election and role of chairperson
- Criteria and process for admittance, removal, and resignation of Committee members
- Training and education required of Committee members
- Frequency of Committee meetings
- Structure of Committee meetings
- Meeting minutes

- Process for resolving disagreements
- Quorum and voting requirements for meeting, approving Policy language, and removing a Committee member or chairperson
- Confidentiality of Committee discussions
- Process for communicating with other church leadership (elders, deacons, pastors, etc.)

After Drafting the Policy

After developing, disseminating, and implementing the Policy, the Committee enters the second phase of ongoing work, with members assuming responsibilities relating to supervision, advisement, compliance, and evaluation. Ideally, the Committee in the second phase is the same as the Committee in the first phase, since this is the group most intimately familiar with the terms of the Policy and the reasoning behind each term. However, if the first group wishes to end their involvement, a second group of capable individuals can form the Committee, so long as there is a process for transferring the key information (e.g., by having the two Committees working together for a few weeks before the first resigns, or keeping one or two individuals from the first Committee on the second as full members, or as-needed advisors).

Depending on your church, the Committee's ongoing work may include,

- Education
- Advisement
- Limited Access Agreements
- Supervision/Monitoring
- Evaluation/Reports/Policy review
- Compliance
- Communication with the congregation

Worksheet: Forming a Committee

A. *Goal:* To form a Child Protection Committee composed of individuals who will guide the church in protecting its children.

B. *Reason:* Protecting children requires knowledge, time, and planning. A standing Committee devoted to protecting children will help the church remain focused on safeguarding its children for the long-term. Committee members are the church's in-house guides to help prevent abuse and respond skillfully to abuse that occurs.

C. *Consider:* As you begin the initial steps of forming a Committee, consider the following questions below:

1. What is the Role and Structure of Your Committee?

a. *Here are five suggestions for areas of child protection that your Committee might oversee.*

1) *Policy Development:* creating a Policy that will provide clear protocols to guide staff and congregants in preventing and responding to child abuse.

2) *Education and Implementation:* communicating the Policy's terms to the entire congregation and developing mechanisms to implement it properly.

3) *Ongoing Evaluation and Maintenance:* meeting regularly as a standing committee in order to evaluate the church's compliance with the Policy and consider revisions to the Policy as necessary; updating the church's leadership and members with Policy revisions.

4) *Advisement:* answering questions about the Policy and advising on child safety issues.

5) *Compliance and Response:* responding to allegations of misconduct or abuse quickly and skillfully.

These suggestions may or may not be practical for your church. Try adding, deleting, or editing our suggestions to come up with a list of roles that fit your context.

» _____

» _____

» _____

» _____

» _____

2. Who Should Be On Your Committee?

 a. What is the minimum/maximum number of people that may be on your Committee?

 Min _____ Max _____

 b. Will you have subcommittees, assign tasks to individual members, or will all members participate in all tasks? (Circle one)

 No Yes

 c. If you answered "Yes" to 2b, by what factor will you divide your subcommittees? (Circle one)

  » Roles (e.g., Policy developer versus Policy reviewer or adviser)
  » Phases (e.g., some will work on Policy development, others on implementation, etc.)
  » Chapters (e.g., each subcommittee will develop Policy language for different chapters)

List the subcommittees and their tasks:

_____

_____

_____

_____

_____

a.   *What expertise do you have in your community?*

»   Child protection professional

»   Child abuse prosecutor _____

»   Victim's advocate _____

»   Mental health professional with expertise treating victims
    or perpetrators of child abuse _____

»   _____

»   Other _____

»   Attorney _____

»   Individual with experience drafting policies _____

»   _____

»   Individual with experience ensuring compliance with poli-
    cies _____

»   Other_____

If you do not have any child protection professional in your
community, consider arranging ongoing consultation with
outside experts. The following organizations often welcome
partnerships with local communities to prevent abuse:

»   GRACE
»   Child advocacy centers
»   Local law enforcement agencies
»   District attorney's offices

b. *Which voices do you want represented on your Committee?*

Below are suggested categories of individuals whose input may be important or helpful to the development of your Policy. Are there others that you would add? In the blanks following each category, list the names of individuals in your community who you believe would be good representatives of these categories. In listing these names, also consider whether these individuals have the personality characteristics you'll list below in "d."

» Church professionals

  - Pastor _____

  - Executive Director _____

  - Youth Director _____

  - Other _____

» Survivor of childhood sexual abuse _____

» Caregiver _____

» Lay leader responsible for ensuring a safe church

  - Chairperson of the Youth Committee _____

  - _____

  - Deacon who oversees the building's security _____

  - _____

  - Member of the church's executive board, elders, or deacons _____

  - Other

c. *What characteristics are important to you in a Committee member?*

Circle those that are essential to your church, cross out those that are not, and add your own to the lines below:

- » Team player
- » Emotionally stable
- » Calm
- » Professional
- » Collaborative
- » Hardworking
- » Dedicated
- » Ethical
- » Moral
- » Honest

- » _____
- » _____
- » _____
- » _____
- » _____
- » _____

d. *What is the process and criteria for admitting an individual to the Committee?*

_____

_____

_____

ACTION STEP

Meet with the individuals on your list and tell them about the
Committee you are forming. Informally or formally screen them to
see if they are individuals who will protect children.

   e. Who are your Committee members?

_____

_____

_____

_____

_____

_____

_____

_____

   f. Who is your Committee Chairperson?

_____

   g. What is your chairperson's role?

_____

_____

_____

_____

3. What is your projected timeline for completing the Policy?

   a. How much time do you project spending on each chapter?

Consider how much time you want to devote to working
through the various chapters in this guide, then fill in your

projected timeline on the lines below. You may need to adjust the timeline once Policy development begins.

Chapter 1: _____

Chapter 2: _____

Chapter 3: _____

Chapter 4: _____

Chapter 5: _____

Chapter 6: _____

Chapter 7: _____

Chapter 8: _____

Chapter 9: _____

Chapter 11: _____

Chapter 12: _____

Chapter 13: _____

Chapter 14: _____

Chapter 15: _____

b. *How often will your Committee meet? (Circle one)*

Biweekly Weekly Bimonthly Monthly Every Two Months

4. What supplementary education will your Committee have? (Check whether required or offered)

	Offered	Required
Online training		
Documentary	.	
Live expert		
Survivor testimony		
Articles, books, or other readings		

5. What preliminary steps will your Committee take before beginning substantive work?

a.   *What trust-building activities will your Committee use at the onset to help foster cohesiveness? Circle those you are interested in or add your own.*

» Listening to a survivor's testimony together

» Watching a movie about child sexual abuse together and discussing it afterwards

» Self-introductions

» Ask members why they chose to be on the Committee (10–20 minutes)

» Ask members to share their thoughts about protecting children (10–20 minutes)

» Allow members of the group share their own direct or indirect experiences of child sexual abuse

» Other_____

b. *List guidelines that your Committee has agreed upon to help set the tone for:*

Communication / interaction style

_____

_____

_____

_____

_____

Approach to dealing with the topic of child sexual abuse

_____

_____

_____

_____

_____

6. What is your Committee's plan for making decisions?

a. *What are your Committee's requirements on quorums and voting?*

Committee Activity	Quorum Required	% Vote Required
Meeting to discuss procedure		N/A
Meeting to discuss content		N/A
Admittance of Committee member		
Removal of Committee member		
Election of Committee chairperson		
Removal of Committee chairperson		
Approval of Policy Language		

Sample Recruitment Email

Dear _____,

Our church is forming a Child Protection Committee that will guide it in taking proactive steps to protect our children from abuse. Would you consider joining this critically important Committee? We believe you bring unique wisdom, experience, sensitivity, and perspective to this project.

The Committee's first job will be to write a Child Protection Policy. The exact meeting schedules are yet to be determined, but we anticipate that the bulk of this process will take place in the coming _____ months. Once this process is complete, the Committee will develop a plan for disseminating the Policy, educating the community about child safety, advising the community when child safety questions or concerns arise, and overseeing the ongoing maintenance and evaluation of this Policy and the church's child safety plan.

If you are interested, there is an initial meeting on _____ to provide you with some background information on child abuse, an overview of this project, and to answer any questions you may have.

By joining this Committee, you will help us to protect our most vulnerable members: our precious children. We hope that you will consider accepting this invitation. Please do not hesitate to contact us with any questions,

Sincerely,

Sample Committee By-Laws

The MISSION of this Child Protection Committee ("Committee") is to develop and maintain a Child Protection Policy ("Policy") that will guide the church in a) preventing opportunities for child abuse and b) responding in the event that child abuse is suspected, witnessed, or reported. The Committee will also advise the church on all matters related to child protection and compliance with the Policy.

The Committee will at all times work to maintain a civil, respectful, and collaborative tone, even and especially, when disagreeing. We operate under the assumption that all on this Committee care deeply about protecting children and are contributing their time, effort, and thoughts in order to benefit children.

> **1. Size.** In the interest of safety and efficiency, this Committee will at all times have a minimum of ____ members and a maximum of ____ members. If at any point the Committee has fewer than ____ members, the Committee will cease meeting to discuss substantive content of the Policy until an additional member(s) is recruited to join the Committee. If it is determined that more than ____ members will be beneficial to the Committee, subcommittees or advisory roles will be created so that meetings to discuss terms of the Policy do not exceed ____ members.
>
> **2. Chairperson.** A chairperson for this Committee will be appointed by the _____. The chairperson's role is to

coordinate meetings, facilitate discussions, disseminate educational resources, and resolve conflicts or blocks to Committee progress. The chairperson's term is indefinite and voluntary. The chairperson may step down from this position at any time after providing notice to the Committee. The Committee may vote to remove the chairperson _____ (*for good cause/without cause*) at any time, according to the terms set out in article 7. Subsequent chairpersons will be selected from within the Committee and elected by a majority vote of the Committee.

3. Admittance and Removal. Admittance onto this Committee is by invitation only. Initial invitations will be extended by _____, and subsequent invitations will be determined by Committee vote, as set forth in article 7 below. Invitations will only be extended to those who have undergone a criminal background check and have met with _____ church staff members or lay leaders for an interview. Committee members may be removed _____ (*for good cause/without cause*) at any time according to the terms set out in article 7 or by _____. Individuals who wish to resign from the Committee may do so at any time and for any reason, with no advance notice required, by sending an email to the entire Committee or to the Committee chairperson.

4. Training. Before beginning to work on a Policy, the Committee will undergo ___ hours of online child-protection training, for which each member will receive a certificate of completion. A copy of each member's certificate will be kept on file in the church. The Committee will also retain an expert on child-protection to address the Committee for an additional ___ hours of training. The online training and expert will be selected by the _____.

5. Meeting Frequency. This Committee will meet _____, but in no event less than _____ until the completion of the Policy. Once the Policy has been completed, the Committee will continue to meet on a regular basis, but in no event less than four times per year.

6. Meeting Structure. All Committee and subcommittee meetings will begin with a prayer and the reading of the Committee mission statement. Minutes will be taken during each meeting and will be stored on an electronic cloud that is shared with the Committee. Once uploaded to the cloud, meeting minutes will be locked for editing, and cannot be revised without a formal request to the committee chairperson. During the Policy development phase, each subcommittee will be assigned two chapters from the *Child Safeguarding Policy Guide*. Subcommittees will be expected to read the relevant chapter in advance of their meetings. At the subcommittee meeting, members will discuss the concepts presented in the workbook and then complete the accompanying activity sheets together. Between subcommittee meetings, members of the subcommittee will use the completed activity sheets to draft and edit language on a shared electronic cloud for inclusion in the Policy. The full Committee must vote before formally accepting language for inclusion in the Policy. Full Committee meetings will be held to approve Policy language drafted by subcommittees and to discuss difficult topics or recurring questions.

7. Quorum and Voting. A quorum of ____ people is required for any non-procedural meeting. A quorum of _____ people and a majority vote are required to approve or disapprove proposed Policy language. A quorum of _____ people and a unanimous vote are required for the removal of any Committee member or chairperson. Any Committee member may call for a vote at any time.

8. Confidentiality. In order for Committee members to feel safe sharing their candid opinions, members may share summaries of meeting content (e.g., to explain to a congregant the reasoning behind specific Policy terms) but may not disclose the identity of individual speakers.

APPENDIX TWO

. . . .

SAMPLE FORMS

Teen Application for a Staff or Volunteer Position

First Name _____ Last Name _____

Social Security Number _____

Date of Birth _____ Age _____

Grade _____

Email Address _____

Home Phone Number _____

Cell Phone Number _____

Address _____

_____

High School Attending _____

Any previous high schools attended _____

Have you ever been suspended or expelled from high school? If so, please list the date and reason for the suspension/expulsion. _____

_____

_____

Have you ever hurt a child? If so, please explain. _____

_____

_____

Has anyone ever accused you of hurting a child? If so, please explain. _____

_____

Please list any and all experience you have had working with or caring for children, whether paid or unpaid. This may include summer jobs, babysitting, volunteering, or caring for younger siblings.

Experience 1

Position _____

Supervisor's name _____

Supervisor's phone # _____

Supervisor's email _____

Start Date _____ End Date _____

Reason for leaving _____

Your role/responsibilities _____

_____

Experience 2

Position _____

Supervisor's name _____

Supervisor's phone # _____

Supervisor's email _____

Start Date _____ End Date _____

Reason for leaving _____

Your role/responsibilities _____

_____

Experience 3

Position _____

Supervisor's name _____

Supervisor's phone # _____

Supervisor's email _____

Start Date _____ End Date _____

Reason for leaving _____

Your role/responsibilities _____

_____

Please list two references below and their contact information. References should be individuals who know you well and can attest to your character and work ethic.

Reference 1

Name _____

Phone _____ Email _____

What is this person's relationship to you? _____

How long have you known this person? _____

Reference 2

Name _____

Phone _____ Email _____

What is this person's relationship to you? _____

How long have you known this person? _____

Describe why you think you would make a good leader. _____

_____

_____

_____

I am interested in working as a youth group leader for the _____ age group. If that is not possible my second preference is the ____ age group, and my third preference, the _____ age group. We will take your preferences into account but will not be able to accommodate all requests. If not being assigned to your preferred age group would cause you to decline an offer to be a group leader, please indicate so here _____.

How did you learn of this position? _____

List any questions you may have or additional information you would like us to know. _____

_____

_____

_____

Sample: Adult Application[1]

The church will store all applications in a secure, locked filing cabinet. The information provided in this application will be kept confidential and shared only as necessary with members of the Search Committee and/or Child Protection Committee. Please attach additional sheets of paper as necessary to answer the questions below.

First Name _____ Last Name _____

Social Security # _____

Driver's License State and # _____

Email Address _____

Home Phone Number _____

Cell Phone Number _____

Please list all addresses you have lived at for the past five years, and your dates of residency.

_____

_____

_____

_____

_____

Position applying for _____

How did you learn of this position? _____

Educational History:

Please list all vocational or certificate programs, colleges, graduate schools, and professional schools you have attended.

Name of school _____

Location _____

Degree/Program _____ Program completed? Yes   No

Dates of attendance _____

Name of school _____

Location _____

Degree/Program _____ Program completed? Yes   No

Dates of attendance _____

Name of school _____

Location _____

Degree/Program _____ Program completed? Yes   No

Dates of attendance _____

Were you ever suspended, expelled, or formally disciplined at any post-high school academic institution for any reason? If so please list the date of the incident, type of discipline, and reason for the discipline. _____

_____

_____

Work Experience:

Please list all previous work history and any and all experience working with children, whether paid or unpaid.

Experience 1

Employer/Organization _____

Start _____ End Date _____

Reason for leaving _____

Position _____

Supervisor's name_____ Supervisor's phone # _____

Supervisor's email _____

Your role/responsibilities _____

Experience 2

Employer/Organization _____

Start _____ End Date _____

Reason for leaving _____

Position _____

Supervisor's name_____ Supervisor's phone # _____

Supervisor's email _____

Your role/responsibilities _____

Experience 3

Employer/Organization _____

Start _____ End Date _____

Reason for leaving _____

Position _____

Supervisor's name_____ Supervisor's phone # _____

Supervisor's email _____

Your role/responsibilities _____

Experience 4

Employer/Organization _____

Start _____ End Date _____

Reason for leaving _____

Position _____

Supervisor's name_____ Supervisor's phone # _____

Supervisor's email _____

Your role/responsibilities _____

Criminal History

Please list any and all criminal arrests or charges, including relevant dates, nature of the offense, conviction, sentence imposed, and any rehabilitation. _____

_____

_____

_____

Have you ever abused or neglected a child? If so, please explain.

_____

_____

_____

_____

Has anyone ever accused you of neglecting or abusing a child or adult? If so, please explain. _____

_____

_____

_____

_____

Have you ever been indicted by an institutional, independent, civil, or criminal investigation of child abuse, neglect, or endangerment in any form? If yes, please list any and all dates of investigation; the individual, organization, or agency conducting the investigation(s); and the finding of the investigation. Please also attach any supporting documents you may have. _____

_____

_____

_____

_____

References:

Please list two references below and their contact information. References should be individuals who have observed or supervised your work with children, who know you well and can attest to your character and work ethic.

Reference 1

Name _____

Phone _____ Email _____

What is this person's relationship to you? _____

How long have you known this person? _____

Reference 2

Name _____

Phone _____ Email _____

What is this person's relationship to you? _____

How long have you known this person? _____

Reference 3

Name _____

Phone _____ Email _____

What is this person's relationship to you? _____

How long have you known this person? _____

List any questions you may have or additional information you would like us to know. _____

_____

_____

_____

Read and initial each item to signify your agreement to comply with the statement should you be offered a position to work or volunteer in our church.

_____ I have received a copy of the church's Child Protection Policy and agree to abide by its terms.

_____ I agree to nurture and protect children and never to engage in behavior that may harm them.

_____ I agree to do my best to prevent abuse and neglect among children involved in church services and activities.

_____ In the event that I observe or hear of any inappropriate behaviors involving children or possible Child Protection Policy violations, I agree to immediately report my observations.

_____ I acknowledge my obligation and responsibility to protect children and agree to report known or suspected abuse of children to appropriate church leaders and city/state authorities in accordance with the Policy.

_____ I understand that the church will not tolerate abuse or other harm of children and I agree to comply in spirit and action with this position.

I understand that it is my duty to provide complete and accurate information and to self-report all prior arrests, charges, investigations, and convictions. I further understand that failure to do so is grounds for denying my application or for later dismissal.

I authorize the church Search Committee to contact any person or organization, whether or not identified in this application, to inquire about my previous employment, education, criminal history, driving records, interactions with youth, personality, character, behavior, work habits, abilities, and other information relevant to the position for which I am applying. I release these references from all liability and responsibility that may result from providing the church with such information. I also authorize the church to request, receive, and evaluate that information, and agree to hold the church harmless from any liability and responsibility that may result from receiving or acting upon information obtained in the screening or hiring process.

I have read, understand, and agree to the above provisions.

Name _____

Signature _____

Date _____

Policy Exception Request Form

Submitted by:

Last Name _____

First Name _____

Phone _____

Email _____

Date _____

Relevant Policy Section _____

Relevant Policy Language _____

_____

_____

Exception Requested _____

_____

_____

Please explain why you believe this exception is necessary.

_____

_____

_____

_____

Is this request ongoing or time limited? If time limited, please list the relevant date(s) below.

____ Ongoing

____ Time limited. Request is for the following date(s)/ program(s) _____

_____

Has anyone on the church's Child Protection Committee or staff preapproved this request?

____ No

____ Yes

Permission received from _____

on _____ .

Notification Form: Necessary Deviation from Policy

Submitted by:

Last Name _____

First Name _____

Phone _____

Email _____

Date _____

Policy Section_____

Policy Language _____

_____

_____

Please list any Policy deviations and explain the circumstances that necessitated these deviations. _____

_____

_____

_____

On what date did this occur? _____.

Who else was present when this occurred? _____

_____

_____

Did anyone specifically object to the deviation? If so, please list their names below: _____

_____

_____

Please share anything else you would like the Child Protection Committee to know. _____

_____

_____

_____

Note: This form is different than the Incident Reporting form, where a third-party reports a violation of the Policy by another. Here the individual who deviated from the Policy is submitting the form himself and explaining the reason why it was necessary to deviate. This sort of person—one who knows the Policy, understands when it needs to be broken, and alerts the Committee when it is—is not the person we are concerned about.

Sample: Child Safety Incident Report*

This form should be used to report to the Child Safety Committee any violation of the Child Safety Policy, boundary violations, disclosures of abuse, child safety concerns, or other behavior or allegations of behavior that might jeopardize the safety of a child. Proof or direct knowledge of a behavior or incident is not necessary to submit this form, and as such some lines on this form may not be applicable to you. Provide whatever information you do have, and where extra space is needed, please continue below the line or attach an additional sheet.

1. Date(s) of incident/behavior, if known _____

2. Name(s) and contact information of child(ren) harmed, potentially harmed, or otherwise adversely impacted by incident/behavior:

_____ Unknown _____ Known (*fill out lines below*)

Child 1 _____

Parent(s) _____

Email _____

Phone _____

Child 2 _____

Parent(s) _____

Email _____

Phone _____

3. Name(s) and contact information of individual(s)—adult or child—who accidentally or intentionally violated the Policy, or otherwise harmed or potentially harmed (the above) child(ren), or who otherwise engaged in concerning behavior.

_____ Unknown _____ Known (*fill out lines below*)

Individual 1 _____

Parent(s) _____

Email _____

Phone _____

Individual 2 _____

Parent(s) _____

Email _____

Phone _____

4. What Policy, if any, was violated? _____

5. Where did the incident/behavior occur? _____

6. Was there an ongoing activity at the time of the incident? If so, what? _____

_____

7. Description of incident/behavior _____

_____

_____

_____

8. Did you witness the concerning incident/behavior firsthand?

_____ Yes _____ No

If not, how did you find out about it? _____

_____

9. Who was present at the time of the incident/behavior?

Name _____

Role in church /Relationship to child _____

Name _____

Role in church /Relationship to child _____

10. Which individuals, other than those listed above, know about this incident? Please include individuals in the church and beyond.

Name _____

Role in church /Relationship to child _____

Name _____

Role in church /Relationship to child _____

11. Please provide the following information for any law enforcement or child protection agencies that were contacted in reference to this incident:

Name of Agency 1 _____

Date(s) of contact _____

Means of communicating with the agency _____

Report #_____

Name(s) of the individual(s) who contacted the agency _____

_____

Name(s) of other individual(s) present when agency was contacted _____

Name of Agency 2 _____

Date(s) of contact _____

Means of communicating with the agency _____

Report #_____

Name(s) of the individual(s) who contacted the agency _____

_____

Name(s) of other individual(s) present when agency was contacted _____

12. Were any child protection professionals or experts, other than those listed above, contacted about this incident? If yes, please indicate the individual(s) or non-governmental agency contacted, the date of the contact, and the result of consult:

Date _____

Consultant_____

Result _____

Date _____

Consultant _____

Result _____

13. What additional steps have been, or will be, taken to respond to this incident/violation? (e.g., other consultations sought, consequences for the actor(s), support for the impacted child(ren), community notification)

(Anticipated) Date _____

Response _____

(Anticipated) Date _____

Response _____

(Anticipated) Date _____

Response _____

(Anticipated) Date _____

Response _____

14. What, if anything, can be done to prevent future similar incidents/violations or improve response procedures?

_____

_____

15. Individual submitting this report:

   Printed Name _____

   Signature _____

   Date _____

Please submit this form to the Child Protection Committee by emailing _____,

mailing it to _____,

or dropping it in the slot of the Committee's private, locked mailbox, located _____.

Sample: Summary of Incident Reports

This form should be used as part of the annual evaluation. Summary information from this form should be included in the Annual Child Protection Report and shared at the general membership meeting.

The information in this summary refers to the following time period:

start date _____ end date _____

1. List the number of reports about child maltreatment or suspicions of child maltreatment made to:

   _____ Police

   _____ District attorney's office

   _____ Child Protective Services

   _____ State child abuse hotline

_____ Federal child abuse hotline

_____ Federal Bureau of Investigation

2. List the number of Incident Reports submitted to the Committee where the perpetrator was a(n):

_____ Adult

_____ Child

3. List the number of reports made to the church's Child Protection Committee with suspicion or knowledge of a child being maltreated by a:

_____ Family member

_____ Staff member

_____ Contractor or subcontractor

_____ Volunteer

_____ Lay leader

_____ Congregant

_____ Visitor

_____ Other

4. List the number of

_____ Child disclosure of abuse to staff, volunteers, or members

_____ Law enforcement investigations

_____ Internal investigations

_____ Independent investigations

_____ Times an applicant wasn't hired because of information uncovered in the screening process

_____ Times an employee or volunteer was suspended or fired because of child protection concerns

_____ Safety-related complaints (other than reports of suspicions or knowledge of abuse) made to the Child Protection Committee

_____ Known violations of the Child Protection Policy by congregants

_____ Known violations of the Child Protection Policy by staff or volunteers

_____ Times a child was seriously injured at a church program

_____ Times a child was seriously injured on the church premises, other than at formal programs

_____ Times a child went missing from a drop-off program

_____ Times a child went missing from the church premises, other than at a drop-off program

5. List the number of incidents you discovered in the process of this evaluation that were not handled in accordance with the terms of the Policy, or had not received the proper follow-up: _____

Have you since rectified these omissions and responded to the incidents as required by the Policy? _____ Yes _____ No

If not, please list the date by which the incident will be resolved.

_____

Evaluator _____

Evaluator's Signature _____

Date _____

Sample: Parent Evaluation of Child Safety in the Church

Our church strives to be a warm environment that is welcoming and safe for all. As part of our efforts to protect the church's children from maltreatment, the Child Safeguarding Committee seeks your feedback on the safety of our children's programming and our compliance with the Child Protection Policy. This survey should take between 5–10 minutes to complete, and is an essential component of our annual child-safety review. Thank you for partnering with us on this critical issue.

The questions in this evaluation refer to the following time period:

start date _____ end date _____

On a scale of 1–5, with 5 being the highest and 1 being the lowest, how safe do you feel your child is in the church

Lobby	1	2	3	4	5	N/A
Hallways & bathrooms	1	2	3	4	5	N/A
Social hall	1	2	3	4	5	N/A
Main sanctuary	1	2	3	4	5	N/A
Outdoor spaces	1	2	3	4	5	N/A
Youth groups	1	2	3	4	5	N/A
Sports teams	1	2	3	4	5	N/A
Youth classes (e.g., karate)	1	2	3	4	5	N/A
Drop-off events (e.g., movie night)	1	2	3	4	5	N/A
Offsite youth trips	1	2	3	4	5	N/A

If you gave a 1 or 2 for any category above, please consider indicating why below.

Comments _____

_____

_____

How well do you think the church adheres to the Child Protection Policy in the following areas?

	Not very well	Well	Very Well	I don't Know
Staff hiring and screening practices				
Volunteer hiring and screening practices				
Registration for participation in youth events				
Drop off and pickup				
Adult-child ratios				
Staff interactions w/ children: verbal, physical, technological				
Off-site events (e.g., trips, events in community or staff members' homes)				
Managing individuals known to pose a risk to children				
Responding to allegations of child abuse or policy violations				
Supporting victims and survivors of child abuse				
Coordinating training and educational events				

If you indicated "Not Very Well" for any category above, please consider indicating why below.

Comments _____

_____

_____

Have you attended any trainings or educational events offered by the church on child safety?

_____ Yes _____ No

If yes, please indicate which one and rate the quality.

	Poor	Adequate	Good	Excellent
Child				
Volunteer				
Parent				
General Congregation				
Internet safety				
Body safety				
Other:				

What were the strengths and weaknesses of the training you attended? How could it have been improved? _____

_____

_____

In what ways do you think the church has been diligent in its protection of children?

_____

_____

In what ways do you think the church can improve its protection of children?

_____

_____

If you wish to provide us with your name and contact information, please do so here. This is optional.

_____

_____

Sample: Cover Letter for Child's Safety Evaluation Form

Dear Parents,

Our church strives to be a warm environment that is welcoming and safe for all. As part of our annual safety evaluation, we would like to provide your children with an opportunity to let us know how we are doing in our efforts to help them feel safe and comfortable in the church. It is our belief that one of the best ways to learn about children is to talk to them, and one of the best ways to protect them is to check in with them directly to make sure that they feel safe. We take your children's protection seriously and are grateful for any feedback they (and you) are comfortable sharing.

This form is designed so that parents can read the questions aloud to younger children and record their answers, or work collaboratively with children who are able to read and write on their own. Older children may prefer to fill out this form in private and submit it on their own. In all instances we recommend explaining to your children our shared goals of keeping them safe and the role this evaluation plays in doing so. This form can also be a helpful tool for you in beginning or continuing a discussion about personal and body safety with your children.

Sincerely,

The Child Protection Committee

Note: If in the process of filling out this form your child discloses information that surprises or worries you (such as that somebody hurt or scared them), remember to stay calm in front of your child. In such a moment, your child will need you to believe, support, and refrain from assigning blame. Avoid asking leading questions and do your best to be a loving listener. The church's Child Protection Committee is here to support you and offer referrals and guidance on how to respond.

Dear Child,

It is important to our community that you feel welcome and comfortable in our church. We want you to enjoy our programming and have fun with your friends. Most importantly, we want to make sure that you feel safe. If someone or something at the church makes you feel bad, uncomfortable, or unsafe, we want to know about it so that we can help fix the problem. And if we are doing a good job, we want to know that too so we can keep up the good work. You do not need to tell us your name when you fill out this form. However, if you would like to tell us your name or would like us to talk to you about any of the things you wrote down on this form, just write that on the form and we'll reach out to you. Thank you for helping us make the church a safer place for you and all children.

Sincerely,

The Child Protection Committee

Sample: Child's Evaluation of Child Safety in the Church

The questions in this evaluation refer to the following time period:

start date _____ end date _____

YOUTH GROUPS AND PROGRAMS

This part of the evaluation is about youth programs. If you do not go to youth programs, skip this section.

1a. Do you think your group leaders and the people who run youth programs do a good job of protecting you and looking out for you?

_____ Yes _____ No

1b. Why or why not?

_____

_____

_____

2. When you are in youth groups or at a youth program, how safe do you feel from:

	Not Very Safe	Safe	Very Safe
Being left out			
Unwanted teasing			
Bullying			
Uncomfortable or inappropriate language			
Being hurt			
Unwanted touch			

3a. Did anyone ever bully you at a youth group or program?

_____ Yes _____ No

3b. Did anyone ever hurt you at a youth group or program?

_____ Yes _____ No

3c. Did anyone ever touch you when you didn't want to be touched at a youth group or program? _____ Yes _____ No

If you answered yes to any of the above questions, please tell us about the situation.

_____

_____

If you answered yes to any of the above questions, did a staff member or volunteer know about the situation?

_____

_____

If a staff member or volunteer knew, what did s/he do? _____

_____

_____

Do you think s/he handled the situation well? _____ Yes _____ No

If not, what do you wish s/he had done instead?_____

_____

_____

CHURCH

The following questions are about anytime you are in the church, even if you are not at a youth program.

4a. Has anyone in the church touched you when you didn't want to be touched? _____ Yes _____ No

4b. If so, please tell us about the situation and the touch.

_____

_____

_____

_____

5a. Are there certain people, times, or spaces in the church that make you feel uncomfortable or unsafe? _____ Yes _____ No

5b. If yes, please indicate who, when, or where, and explain why you feel uncomfortable or unsafe.

_____

_____

_____

_____

6. What are some things the Child Protection Committee can do to make you feel safer at the church?

_____

_____

6. If you have concerns that we have not asked about, or have suggestions, questions, or anything else that you would like to share with the Child Protection Committee, please do so here:

_____

_____

_____

_____

If you wish to provide us with your name and contact information please do so here. This is optional.

_____

Sample Youth Leader Evaluation Form

This sample form was created with teen youth leaders in mind, but can be adapted for any staff/volunteer.

Name and title/responsibility of individual being evaluated

_____

The questions in this evaluation refer to the following time period:

start date _____ end date _____

Please rate the staff/volunteer on the following qualities:

	Poor	Adequate	Good	Excellent	Cannot Judge or N/A
Attendance					
Preparation					
Following rules					
Initiative					
Creativity					
Problem solving					
Frustration tolerance					
Leadership					
Responsibility					
Positivity					
Child protection					
Interaction with children					
Interaction with parents					
Interaction with coworkers					
Interaction with supervisors					

Please elaborate on the above qualities, and others not included above, by:

listing some of the areas in which this youth leader excels.

_____

_____

listing some of the areas in which this youth leader needs improvement.

_____

_____

Has this leader ever expressed hesitancy in protecting children or following the Policy? Yes/No

If yes, please elaborate: _____

_____

_____

List any additional information that is relevant in evaluating this youth leader.

_____

_____

Evaluator _____

Evaluator's Signature _____

Date _____

Quarterly Review: Limited Access Agreements

This form should be used during the Child Safety Committee's quarterly reviews of all individual files. Individuals with files include those who have been the subject of a Limited Access Agreement. After completing this form, it should be added to the individual's file.

Name of Individual _____

The questions in this review refer to the following time period:

start date _____ end date _____

1. Please list any new information that might mitigate this person's risk. _____

_____

_____

2. Please list any new information that might contribute to this person's risk. _____

_____

_____

3. This individual:

_____ Has been banned from our church and

    _____ has not attempted entrance or loitered on church property since the ban.

    _____ *has* attempted entrance, did enter, or loitered on church property on these date(s) _____

    _____

_____ Has a Limited Access Agreement

    _____ and has been compliant with its terms.

    _____ and has *not* been compliant with its terms. The following steps have been, or will be, taken in response to this individual's noncompliance:

    _____

    _____

    These steps have been, or will be completed on

    _____.

_____ Does not have a Limited Access Agreement

    _____ and we believe one is not warranted because _____

    _____

_____ but we believe one is warranted going forward because _____.

4. If applicable, please list any revisions you recommend to this individual's Limited Access Agreement:

_____

_____

Reviewer _____

Reviewer's Signature _____

Date _____

Sample: Committee's Evaluation of Child Safety in the Church

The questions in this evaluation refer to the following time period:

start date _____ end date _____

1. List the dates, topics, audiences, and cost of any child protection trainings or educational programs that the church hosted.

	Date	Topic	Audience	Cost
1				
2				
3				
4				
5				

2. What areas of the policy seem to be consistently violated or pose the most challenge to implement? Why do you think this may be?

Area	Explanation

3. Which departments in the church excel at following the Policy? Why do you think this is?

_____

_____

_____

_____

4. Which departments have the most difficulty following the Policy? Why do you think this is?

_____

_____

_____

_____

5. Are there resources, personnel, funding, or structural changes ("Items") that would be necessary ("N") or helpful ("H") in making the church safer for children?

N/H	Item	Why would this make the church safer for children?

6. What policies does the Child Protection Committee recommend revising? Why?

_____

_____

_____

_____

7. What new policies does the Child Protection Committee recommend adding? Why?

_____

_____

_____

_____

8. In what ways has the church supported known victims or survivors of child abuse?

_____

_____

_____

9. In what ways is the church succeeding in protecting children? Give evidence when possible.

_____

_____

_____

_____

10. In what ways can the church improve its protection of children?

_____

_____

_____

_____

APPENDIX THREE

. . . .

EMPOWERING CHILDREN

While it is never children's job to protect themselves, educating children in an age-appropriate manner can bring great benefits. Your church should consider educational programs for children that communicate about your Child Protection Policy so that children are aware of the rules put in place to protect them and understand what to do if someone violates the rules. Your church can also educate children in general body safety.

Policy Education

Certain terms of your church's Policy may affect children. For example, children in the nursery may be used to sitting on an adult's lap, but the Policy now prohibits lap-sitting. Educating children about relevant terms can help them understand changes in their routines. It is a good idea to place child-friendly signs in youth spaces reminding everyone of the relevant terms of the Policy. Another way to communicate the policies and create the signs is to solicit the children's involvement. An educator or trainer might initiate a discussion with a youth group about creating safe spaces and ask children what things would help them to feel safe. The ideas generated by the children can be listed on a poster board. These conversations help children think about their personal safety, and seeing the rules they suggested hanging on their classroom wall lets them know that their voices play an important role in determining Policy.

This can be an empowering experience for children and helps to encourage the very messages inherent in child protection—trust your own voice and speak up. This process should be repeated at the start of every year, and the group should review the rules periodically throughout the year. In addition, just as with adults in the congregation, children should be reminded of the rules informally as they come up, so that the rules become part of the group culture.

Informal, Low-Key Ways to Communicate Your Policy to Children

The Policy rules alluded to here are samples that may or may not be appropriate for your church, and are referenced here as an example of a low-key way to remind children about a Policy term rather than a prescription of what your Policy should include.

- We don't sit on laps in groups, but I would love for you to sit next to me in the prayer circle.
- Ethan, please don't lower the shades. We keep the shades open so that others can see what's going on in here and know that you are all okay and having fun.
- Shay, Rachel told you that she doesn't want you to touch her right now. Maybe she'll want a hug later.
- Sarah, I know that you like talking to Ben, but he's using the bathroom right now and we need to give him privacy. You can talk to him from outside the bathroom or wait until he's finished.
- David looks like he can use some space right now. Let's everyone take one step back and make sure to respect each other's personal space.
- Hey Sam, that joke is not appropriate. If you want to compliment Ariel, you can tell her she looks nice today, but please do not comment on other people's bodies.
- Hayden, I bet Ron would like to be in your picture, but just to make sure, please go ask his permission before you take it.
- Ariel, thanks for telling me that you're finished using the toilet. I'll give you some tissues, but you'll have to wipe yourself. Do the best you can and if you need help we'll ask your parents.

Body-Safety Education

A crucial step in preventing child abuse involves educating children about their bodies, sex, and abuse in an age-appropriate manner. Sometimes caregivers are reluctant to discuss these issues because they believe they are inappropriate or do not want to scare their children. However, our society is replete with subtle and not-so-subtle messages about bodies and sex, and children will learn about these topics, if not from other children, then simply by living in this world. It is better that children receive a calm, informative, and age-appropriate introduction to these topics from their caregivers than from peers, media, or a child abuser.[1] Churches may wish to become involved in this step of prevention by inviting an expert to assist caregivers in talking to their children, providing curricula and other resources for caregivers, or hosting educational classes for children on this topic. Churches participating in GRACE's Certification will be provided with a curriculum. In addition, a church may wish to post signs throughout their youth spaces, reinforcing some of these ideas. A sample sign is included below:[2]

My Body Safety Rules

My body is my body and it belongs to me!

I can say, "No!" if I don't want to kiss or hug someone. I can give them a high five, shake their hand, or blow them a kiss. I am the boss of my body and what I say goes!

I have a Safety Network

These are five adults I trust. I can tell these people anything and they will believe me.

If I feel worried, scared, or unsure, I can tell someone on my Safety Network how I am feeling and why I feel this way.

Early Warning Signs

If I feel frightened or unsafe I may sweat a lot, get a sick tummy, become shaky, and my heart might beat really fast.

These feelings are called my Early Warning Signs. If I feel this way about anything, I must tell an adult on my Safety Network straightaway.

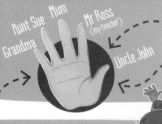

Aunt Sue   Mum   Mr Ross (my teacher)

Grandma   Uncle John

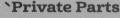

Secrets

I should never keep secrets that make me feel bad or uncomfortable. If someone asks me to keep a secret that makes me feel bad or unsafe, I must tell an adult on my Safety Network straightaway!

Private Parts

My private parts are the parts of my body under my bathing suit. I always call my private parts by their correct names. No one can touch my private parts. No one can ask me to touch their private parts. And no one should show me pictures of private parts. If any of these things happen, I must tell a trusted adult on my Safety Network straightaway.

Original concept The Mama Bear Effect
© UpLoad Publishing Pty Ltd   For Body Safety resources go to **e2epublishing.info**

Teaching Children about Personal Space

Children should be taught to respect the personal space of others. This topic should be discussed and practiced at home, at school, and in the church. In the context of learning to respect the boundaries of others, children should be taught to speak up if they believe that their own boundaries are being encroached upon. They should feel comfortable and entitled to demand respect for their personal space in a polite manner from other children (e.g., siblings, cousins, or friends) as well as from adults (e.g., caregivers, teachers, and pastors). Children should be taught that if someone violates their personal space or touches them in a way that is uncomfortable (e.g., gives them an "uh-oh" feeling), confusing, or simply not okay with them,[3] they should tell an adult whom they trust. Children should be taught to continue telling a different adult until someone believes them and takes care of the problem. Assist children in constructing a list of three to five trustworthy adults to whom they can turn.

In one church's school, a seventh grader was the last student remaining in the classroom when her teacher decided to test the waters. He approached her from behind and began playing with her ponytail and massaging her shoulders. The child told the principal about the incident and he spoke to the pastor. While unfortunately no further protective actions were taken and the teacher continued to touch other children, the teacher never again touched the child who reported his behavior. Children who are taught to report uncomfortable touch immediately—the way this student did—protect themselves from future more intrusive advances.

Adults, especially caregivers, should model respect for a child's boundaries. Questions such as "I would love to hug you right now, would that be okay?" and "Do you have any kisses to share with Grandpa today?" teach children that they are in charge of the physical affection they give and receive, and normalizes their right to decline this affection. Caregivers should affirm their children's right to autonomy over their own body and personal space when interacting with family, friends, and community members. For instance, if an adult at a church event ruffles a child's hair and the child is uncomfortable, caregivers should encourage the child to say so and request that the adult stop. Caregivers should practice respectful language with their children and stand up for their children if an adult is dismissive or ignores the child's request. These are critical tools that help children. Moreover, caregivers who advocate for their child in this way send a clear message to any adults who may be considering abusing their child: boundary violations and disrespect for this child's wishes will not be tolerated. This is a child who knows his/her rights, demands compliance, and has been trained to report boundary violations.

Ways to Affirm a Child's Right to Personal Space

- Teach children that they have permission to say "NO" to unwanted touch from any child or adult.
- Don't demand physical affection from children for yourself or others (e.g., "Give Aunt Sara a kiss").
- Respect the boundaries children set as much as possible and always comply with requests to cease touch (e.g., "I'm stopping tickling you now because you asked me to. I'll be glad to start again when you're ready.").

Creating a Safe Space

In order for children to feel comfortable reporting abuse, they need to have a safe space where it is okay to talk about anything. Churches can help create this space by hosting safety trainings for children and caregivers. Caregivers and educators also create this space—well in advance of a crisis—during the many routine conversations they have with children. When children are talking to you, do your best to express interest in their feelings and be supportive of their ideas. Encourage children to share concerns or problems with you, and demonstrate that you are a reliable advocate.

Instruct children that if an adult lies or asks them to keep a secret, they should immediately tell you or another trustworthy adult. Also, give children explicit permission to disobey an adult if the adult orders them to break the rules or do something wrong. Promise children that if they come to you with these sorts of problem, you will believe them, you will not blame them, they will not be in trouble, and you will help them. Finally, tell children that it is your job to protect them and that when they tell you that something is bothering them, they help you do your job.

Suggested Topics for Inclusion in Children's Educational Safety Events

1. Teach children the names of their body parts
2. Children have the right to deny affection or touch—their body is their own
3. What type of touching (e.g., sexual and physical abuse defined in age-appropriate manner), looking (e.g., in-person and videos), and talking (e.g., emotional, psychological, and spiritual abuse, lewd language, invasive questions, sharing intimate information) are off limits. Note:
   - Discussions of good/bad touch and stranger-danger are outdated
   - It should be made clear that it is not the child's fault if someone violates these rules
   - This list will need to be adapted for different age groups
4. Children have a right to say no to anyone who asks them to break these rules
5. Adults should not ask children to keep secrets
6. Help children construct a list of five people to tell if someone violates the rules
7. Discuss blocks children might face in determining whether or not to disclose abuse
8. Outline the reaction children can expect from identified "Safe people" in the church (e.g., I will believe you; I will protect you; you will not be blamed or punished)
9. Internet safety

· · · ·

ACKNOWLEDGMENTS

This important resource could never have been completed without the tireless contribution of so many who have given their lives in varying ways to make our faith communities safer for children and more welcoming to those who have been abused. We would do an injustice by attempting to acknowledge by name all those who fit in that category—and we'd no doubt run out of pages. However, there are a few we want to specifically acknowledge and without whom we could never have completed this monumental task. Victor Vieth is not only a dear friend, but is one of the greatest child advocates alive today. Without his experience and expertise, this book would never have been written. Victor's tireless words of encouragement kept us going with his gentle but constant reminder that what we do is for the children. We must never forget that. We also want to thank Beth Hart for her amazing gift as an editor. She did a masterful job in transforming a lengthy and sometimes clunky manuscript into this organized and user-friendly resource. Beth's amazing work along with her constant optimism inspired both of us forward to completion. We are also grateful for the much needed pastoral feedback from Mike Sloan. His insights from a pastor's perspective were invaluable for a book written to faith communities. Lastly, this book would have never been written without the wisdom and inspiration provided by so many abuse survivors around the world. We continue to have so much to learn from these amazing heroes of our time.

....

ENDNOTES

Introduction

1. The guide will focus primarily upon child sexual abuse, but where applicable, it will address other forms of child maltreatment.

2. Anna Salter, *Predators, Pedophiles, Rapists, and Other Sex Offenders: Who They Are, How They Operate, and How We Can Protect Ourselves and Our Children* (New York: Basic Books, 2003), 6.

Chapter One

1. For the purposes of this book, the term "child" includes both young children and teens.

2. Find your state's definition of abuse on the United States Department of Health and Human Services, Child Welfare Information Gateway (2014), "State Statutes: Definitions of child abuse and neglect," retrieved from www.childwelfare.gov/topics/systemwide/laws-policies/statutes/define/ and your state's age of consent under "Statutory Rape, Criminal Offenses: Sexual Intercourse with Minors," retrieved from http://aspe.hhs.gov/hsp/08/sr/statelaws/summary.shtml.

3. V. J. Felitti, and R. F. Anda, "The Relationship of Adverse Childhood Experiences to Adult Medical Disease, Psychiatric Disorders and Sexual Behavior: Implications for Healthcare," in *The Impact of Early Life Trauma on Health and Disease: The Hidden Epidemic*, ed. Ruth A. Lanius, Eric Vermetten, and Clare Pain (Cambridge: Cambridge University Press: 2010).

4. Heather A. Turner, David Finkelhor, and Richard Ormrod, "Poly-Victimization in a National Sample of Children and Youth," *American*

Journal of Preventative Medicine 38, no. 3 (2010); David Finkelhor, Richard K. Ormrod, Heather A. Turner, *Journal of Child Abuse and Neglect* 31, no. 7 (2007).

5. David Finkelhor, Heather A. Turner, S. Hamby, and R. Ormrod, *Polyvictimization: Children's Exposure to Multiple Types of Violence, Crime, and Abuse* (Washington, DC: US Department of Justice, Office of Juvenile Justice and Delinquency Prevention, October 2011), retrieved from www.ncjrs.gov/pdffiles1/ojjdp/235504.pdf.

6. N. D. Vogeltanz, et al., "Prevalence and Risk Factors for Childhood Sexual Abuse in Women: National Survey Findings," *Child Abuse & Neglect* 23 (1999): 579–92; D. Finkelhor, and L. Baron, "Risk Factors for Child Sexual Abuse," *Journal of Interpersonal Violence* 1 (1994): 31–53.

7. Finkelhor, Turner, Hamby, Ormrod, *Polyvictimization*, retrieved from www.ncjrs.gov/pdffiles1/ojjdp/235504.pdf.

8. Child Welfare Information Gateway, *Long-Term Consequences of Child Abuse and Neglect* (Washington, DC: US Department of Health and Human Services, Children's Bureau, 2013), retrieved from https://www.childwelfare.gov/pubpdfs/long_term_consequences.pdf.

9. Some in the child-protection field use the term "sexual abuse" only when referring to molestation occurring within a family unit (i.e., biological or custodial) and the term "sexual victimization" when referring to molestation perpetrated by those outside the family unit (e.g., acquaintances or strangers). For an example, see footnote 2 in J. Clemente, *Analysis of the Special Investigative Counsel Report and the Crimes of Gerald A. Sandusky and Education Guide to the Identification and Prevention of Child Sexual Victimization* (2013), retrieved from www.paterno.com/Resources/Docs/CLEMENTE_FINAL_REPORT_2-7-2013.pdf. Since the term "sexual abuse" is more widely used by the general public, this guide will use sexual abuse to refer to all types of sexual victimization.

10. H. N. Snyder, *Sexual Assault of Young Children as Reported to Law Enforcement: Victim, Incident, and Offender Characteristics* (Washington, DC: Department of Justice, National Center for Juvenile Justice, 2000), retrieved from www.bjs.gov/content/pub/pdf/saycrle.pdf.

11. For a more detailed discussion on factors impacting reported prevalence of child sexual abuse, see: E. M. Douglas, and D. Finkelhor, "Childhood Sexual Abuse Fact Sheet," 2005, Crimes Against Children Research Center, retrieved from http://cola.unh.edu/sites/cola.

unh.edu/files/departments/Crimes%20Against%20Children%20Re-search%20Center/pdf/topics/childhoodSexualAbuseFactSheet.pdf.

12.   Centers for Disease Control and Prevention, "Adverse Child-hood Experiences Study: Major Findings," (2016), retrieved from www.cdc.gov/violenceprevention/acestudy/about.html. See also: S. R. Dube, R. F. Anda, C. L. Whitfield, D. W. Brown, V. J. Felitti, M. Dong, and W. H. Giles, "Long-Term Consequences of Childhood Sexual Abuse by Gender of Victim," *American Journal of Preventive Medicine* 28 (2005): 430–38, retrieved from www.ajpmonline.org/article/S0749-3797(05)00078-4/fulltext.

13.   Oftentimes, the terms *assault* and *battery* are used interchange-ably. However, if used as legal terms, many jurisdictions consider them to be separate offenses. In such jurisdictions, a battery usually requires some form of physical contact while an assault does not. Sometimes assault is defined as an incomplete battery.

14.   See generally, J. E. B. Myers, *Myers on Evidence of Interpersonal Vi-olence*, 5th ed. (New York: Wolters Kluwer, 2011); V. I. Vieth, "The Inter-section of Law & Religion in Cases of Corporal Punishment," Gundersen National Child Protection Training Center Newsletter (2015), retrieved from http://nfpcar.org/NCPTC/Spanking_Law_Religion_VictorV.pdf.

15.   For an excellent discussion of this topic, see V. I. Vieth, "From Sticks to Flowers: Guidelines for Child Protection Professionals Work-ing with Parents Using Scripture to Justify Corporal Punishment," *Wil-liam Mitchell Law Review* 40 (2014): 907–42, retrieved from https://www.gundersenhealth.org/app/files/public/2781/NCPTC-From-Sticks-to-Flowers.pdf.

16.   Centers for Disease Control and Prevention, "Adverse Child-hood Experiences Study: Major Findings," (2016), retrieved from www.cdc.gov/violenceprevention/acestudy/about.html.

17.   David Finkelhor, H. Turner, R. Ormrod, S. Hamby, and K. Kracke, *Children's Exposure to Violence: A Comprehensive National Sur-vey* (Washington, DC: U.S. Department of Justice, Office of Juvenile Justice and Delinquency Prevention, 2009), retrieved from https://www.ncjrs.gov/pdffiles1/ojjdp/227744.pdf.

18.   A. J. Sedlak, J. Mettenburg, M. Basena, I. Petta, K. McPher-son, A. Greene, and S. Li, *Fourth National Incidence Study of Child Abuse and Neglect (NIS–4): Report to Congress* (Washington, DC: U.S.

Department of Health and Human Services, Administration for Children and Families, 2010), retrieved from www.acf.hhs.gov/sites/default/files/opre/nis4_report_congress_full_pdf_jan2010.pdf.

19. C. P. Bradshaw, et al., "Psychological Maltreatment" in *Chadwick's Child Maltreatment*, ed., D. L. Chadwick, A. P. Giardino, R. Alexander, J. D. Thackeray, and D. Esernio-Jenssen, 4th ed. (Florissant, MO: STM Learning, Inc., 2014), vol. 2.

20. Department of Health and Human Services, "An overview of the Victorian Child Safety Standards State of Victoria," (Melbourne, Australia: Department of Health and Human Services, 2015), retrieved from http://www.dhs.vic.gov.au/__data/assets/word_doc/0005/955598/An-overview-of-the-Victorian-child-safe-standards_20170324.doc.

21. Centers for Disease Control and Prevention, "Adverse Childhood Experiences Study: Major Findings," (2016), retrieved from www.cdc.gov/violenceprevention/acestudy/about.html.

22. A. H. Claussen and P. M. Crittenden, "Physical and psychological maltreatment: relations among types of maltreatment," *Child Abuse Neglect* 15 (1991):5–18.

23. This definition has been adapted from SAR High School's Policy. To see the definition as originally articulated in their Policy, visit https://drive.google.com/file/d/0B59GjfoOz40tUmhJYkFORC1mM2FncUEwR3VyWWZ4TEhoUGZ3/view?usp=sharing.

24. The US Department of Health and Human Services reports that in one year (2005–2006), more than 1.25 million children in the US were maltreated; 61% of those maltreated children were neglected and 44% were abused. See: Sedlak, et al., *Fourth National Incidence Study of Child Abuse and Neglect (NIS–4)*, retrieved from www.acf.hhs.gov/sites/default/files/opre/nis4_report_congress_full_pdf_jan2010.pdf.

25. See generally, T. Bryant-Davis, M. U. Ellis, E. Burke-Maynard, N. Moon, P. A. Counts, and G. Anderson, "Religiosity, Spirituality, and Trauma Recovery in the Lives of Children and Adolescents," *Professional Psychology: Research & Practice* 43 (2012): 306–14; D. F. Walker, H. W. Reid, T. O'Neil, and L. Brown, "Changes in Personal Religion/Spirituality during and after Childhood Abuse: A Review and Synthesis," *Psychological Trauma Theory Research Practice and Policy* 1 (2009): 130–45; D. M. Elliott, "The Impact of Christian Faith on the Prevalence and Sequelae of Sexual Abuse," *Journal of Interpersonal Violence* 9 (1994): 95–108.

26. Christa Brown, *This Little Light* (Cedarburg, WI: Foremost Press, 2009), 11.

27. Ibid., 12.

28. Bryant-Davis, et. al., "Religiosity, Spirituality, and Trauma Recovery in the Lives of Children and Adolescents," 306–14; Walker, Reid, O'Neil, and Brown, "Changes in Personal Religion/Spirituality during and after Childhood Abuse," 130–45; Elliott, "The Impact of Christian Faith on the Prevalence and Sequelae of Sexual Abuse," 95–108.

29. This definition has been adapted from the SAR High School Policy. To see the definition as originally articulated in their Policy, visit: https://drive.google.com/file/d/0B59GjfoOz40tUmhJYkFOR C1mM2FncUEwR3VyWWZ4TEhoUGZ3/view?usp=sharing.

30. United States Department of Health and Human Services, Child Welfare Information Gateway. (2013). What Is Child Abuse and Neglect? Recognizing the Signs and Symptoms. Retrieved from www. childwelfare.gov/pubpdfs/whatiscan.pdf.

31. This guide uses [Faith Church] as a placeholder. As you assemble your church's policy, fill in with your church's name.

Chapter Two

1. The bullet lists have been adapted from Prevent Child Abuse America. See "Recognizing Child Abuse: What Parents Should Know," retrieved from http://www.preventchildabuse.org/images/docs/recognizingchildabuse-whatparentsshouldknow.pdf.

2. While the notion of modesty may cause children to be bashful about changing (especially girls), extreme reactions, particularly in very young children, may be cause for concern.

3. W. N. Friedrich, J. Fisher, D. Broughton, M. Houston, C. R. Shafran, "Normative Sexual Behavior in Children: A Contemporary Sample," *Pediatrics* 101 (1998): 9, retrieved from http://pediatrics.aap-publications.org/content/101/4/e9.full.

4. Ibid. See Tables 3 and 4 for normative sexual behavior categorized by gender. The American Academy of Pediatrics and the Prince Edwards Island government have also released helpful guides for differentiating between normal and concerning sexual behaviors. See N. D. Kellogg, "Clinical Report—The Evaluation of Sexual Behaviors in Children," *American Academy of Pediatrics* 124 (2009): 992–98, retrieved from

http://pediatrics.aappublications.org/content/pediatrics/124/3/992.full.
pdf and The Provincial Child Sexual Abuse Advisory Committee, *Children's Sexual Behaviours: A Parent's Guide* (Prince Edward Island, Canada, 2013), retrieved from www.gov.pe.ca/photos/original/CSS_CSBPGEn.pdf.

5. S. R. Dube, R. F. Anda, C. L. Whitfield, D. W. Brown, V. J. Felitti, M. Dong, and W. H. Giles, "Child Sexual Abuse: Consequences and Implications," *Journal of Pediatric Health Care* 24 (2005): 358–64, retrieved from http://www.jpedhc.org/article/S0891-5245(09)00208-9/pdf; See also, S. R. Dube, et. al., "Long-Term Consequences of Childhood Sexual Abuse by Gender of Victim," 430–38, retrieved from www.ajpmonline.org/article/S0749-3797(05)00078-4/fulltext.

Chapter Three

1. Child Welfare Information Gateway, *Long-Term Consequences of Child Abuse and Neglect*, retrieved from https://www.childwelfare.gov/pubpdfs/long_term_consequences.pdf.

2. G. Horner, "Child Sexual Abuse: Consequences and Implications," 358–64; C. Tremblay, M. Hebert, and C. Piche, "Coping Strategies and Social Support as Mediators of Consequences in Child Sexual Abuse Victims," *Child Abuse & Neglect* 23 (1999): 929–45.

3. The ten adverse childhood experiences studied were: sexual abuse, emotional abuse, physical abuse, exposure to a household member who was a substance abuser, mentally ill, or incarcerated, and being the child of a victimized mother, or separated parents. See: Centers for Disease Control and Prevention, "Adverse Childhood Experiences Study: Major Findings," (2016), retrieved from www.cdc.gov/violenceprevention/acestudy/about.html.

4. See: V. J. Felitti, and R. F. Anda, "The Relationship of Adverse Childhood Experiences to Adult Medical Disease, Psychiatric Disorders and Sexual Behavior: Implications for Healthcare," in *The Impact of Early Life Trauma on Health and Disease: The Hidden Epidemic*, ed. Ruth A. Lanius, Eric Vermetten and Clare Pain (Cambridge: Cambridge University Press, 2010).

5. Centers for Disease Control and Prevention, "Adverse Childhood Experiences Study: Major Findings," (2016), retrieved from www.cdc.gov/violenceprevention/acestudy/about.html.

6. See Felitti, and Anda, "The Relationship of Adverse Childhood Experiences,"; V. J. Felitti, R. F. Anda, D. Nordenberg, D. F. Williamson, A. M. Spitz, V. Edwards, M. P. Koss, J. S. Marks, "Relationship of Childhood Abuse and Household Dysfunction to Many of the Leading Causes of Death in Adults. The Adverse Childhood Experiences (ACE) Study," *American Journal of Preventive Medicine* 14 (1998): 245–58; Academy on Violence and Abuse (AVA), Dr. Vincent Felleti's overview of ACE study, retrieved from www.avahealth.org/ace_study/ace_study_dvd_institutional_ license/ace_study_summary_14. html; S. R. Dube, et. al., "Long-Term Consequences of Childhood Sexual Abuse by Gender of Victim," 430–38. Retrieved from www. ajpmonline.org/article/S0749-3797(05)00078-4/fulltext; Centers for Disease Control Child Maltreatment, "Consequences," retrieved from www.cdc.gov/violenceprevention/childmaltreatment/consequences. html; L. Starecheski, *Can family secrets make you sick?* (NPR News: All Things, Considered, 2015), retrieved from www.npr.org/blogs/ health/2015/03/02/377569413/can-family-secrets-make-you-sick.

7. Felitti, and Anda, "The Relationship of Adverse Childhood Experiences."

8. T. L. Gall, V. Basque, M. Damasceno-Scott, and G. Vardy, "Spirituality and the Current Adjustment of Adult Survivors of Childhood Sexual Abuse," *Journal for the Scientific Study of Religion* 46 (2007): 101–17; R. Lawson, B. Drebing, G. Berg, A. Vincelette, and W. Penk, "The Long Term Impact of Child Abuse on Religious Behavior and Spirituality in Men," *Child Abuse & Neglect* 22 (1998): 369–80.

9. See D. F. Walker, H. W. Reid, T. O'Neill, and L. Brown, "Changes in Personal Religion/Spirituality during Recovery from Childhood Abuse: A Review and Synthesis, *Psychological Trauma: Theory, Research, Practice, and Policy* 1 (2009): 130–45.

10. See V. I. Vieth, and B. Tchividjian, *When the Child Abuser Has a Bible: Investigating Child Maltreatment Sanctioned or Condoned by a Religious Leader* (Lynchburg, VA: Liberty University School of Law, 2011), retrieved from http://digitalcommons.liberty.edu/cgi/viewcontent.cgi?article=1053&context=lusol_fac_pubs.

11. S. J. Rossetti, "The Impact of Child Sexual Abuse on Attitudes toward God and the Catholic Church," *Child Abuse & Neglect* 19 (1995): 1469–81; V. I. Vieth, "When Faith Hurts: Overcoming Spirituality-

Based Blocks and Problems," *Centerpiece* 2 (2010): 1–6, retrieved from www.gundersenhealth.org/app/files/public/1423/CenterPiece-Vol-2-Issue-10.pdf; T. Doyle, "The Spiritual Trauma Experienced by Victims of Sexual Abuse by Catholic Clergy," *Pastoral Psychology* 58 (2009): 239–60.

Chapter Four

1. Kenneth V. Lanning, *Child Molesters: A Behavioral Analysis*, 5th ed. (National Center. for Missing and Exploited Children, 2011), 51, retrieved from http://www.missingkids.com/en_US/publications/NC70.pdf; see also United States v. Romero, 189 F.3d 576, 582–83 (7th Cir. 1999) (admitting the testimony of an FBI expert on child sexual abuse to explain the methods and techniques used by certain child molesters).

2. Kenneth V. Lanning, *Child Molesters: A Behavioral Analysis*, 5th ed. (National Center. for Missing and Exploited Children, 2011), 57 ("The pedophile will almost always have a method of gaining access to children.").

3. Ibid., 58 ("[A] pedophile must know how to manipulate and control children."); Ibid., 68 ("Child molesters control their victims in a variety of ways.").

4. As used herein, "instrumental physical force" refers to the real or threatened force necessary to accomplish the sexual assault or molestation. See, e.g., Marshall v. State, 832 N.E.2d 615, 619 (Ind. Ct. App. 2005) (documenting how a child was sexually abused by a stranger who forced the child to comply after threatening the child and the child's younger brother with a knife); Lana Stermac, Kathryn Hall & Marianne Henskens, "Violence Among Child Molesters," *Sex Res.* 26 (1989): 240–44, 266–71.

5. John Conte, Steven Wolf, and Tim Smith, "What Sexual Offenders Tell Us About Prevention Strategies," *Child Abuse and Neglect* 13 (1989): 293–301.

6. In applying the factors for each type of child molester below, the factor with the most significance for that particular child molester type will be applied first.

7. Kenneth V. Lanning, *Child Molesters: A Behavioral Analysis*, 5th ed. (National Center for Missing and Exploited Children, 2011), 9. Though these categories are distinctively defined, it is important to note that they should be considered on a continuum rather than independent from one another. For example, an acquaintance molester may

end up marrying the child's parent and becoming an intra-familial molester. Ibid., 10 ("The offender gradually moves from being a stranger using force to an acquaintance using seduction to a father-like or domestic figure using a family-like bond.").

8. Ibid.

9. See generally David Finkelhor, *Sourcebook on Child Sexual Abuse* (1986); Salter, *Predators*; Gene Abel, "Self-Reported Sex Crimes of Non-incarcerated Paraphiliacs," *Interpersonal Violence* 3, no.1 (1987). The US Department of Justice reports that 34 percent of sexual offenses against children are perpetrated by family members, close to 60 percent are perpetrated by acquaintances, and only 7 percent are perpetrated by strangers. See Table 6 in H. N. Snyder, (2000). *Sexual assault of young children as reported to law enforcement: Victim, incident, and offender characteristics*, Department of Justice, National Center for Juvenile Justice, Washington, D.C. U.S., retrieved from www.bjs.gov/content/pub/pdf/saycrle.pdf.

10. See, e.g., Marshall v. State, 832 N.E.2d 615, 619 (Ind. Ct. App. 2005) (documenting how a child was sexually abused by a stranger who forced the child to comply after threatening the child and the child's younger brother with a knife).

11. Lana Stermac, Kathryn Hall, Marianne Henskens, "Violence Among Child Molesters," *Sex Res.* 26 (1989): 450, 453.

12. APRI's National Center for Prosecution of Child Abuse, *Am. Prosecutors Res. Inst., Investigation and Prosecution of Child Abuse*, 3d ed. (Thousand Oaks, CA: Sage Publications, Inc., 2004).

13. See, e.g., Hennagan v. Dep't of Highway Safety and Motor Vehicles, 467 So. 2d 748, 749 (Fla. Dist. Ct. App. 1985) (using his position of authority, a police officer gained access to and molested a child).

14. Press Release, Nancy A. McBride, Nat'l Safety Dir., Nat'l Ctr. for Missing & Exploited Children, Child Safety is More Than a Slogan: "Stranger-Danger" Warnings Not Effective at Keeping Kids Safer, retrieved from http://www.missingkids.com/en_US/publications/PDF10A.pdf. (noting that the phrase "stranger danger" has become "so pervasive in our culture that it has become part of the lexicon").

15. See Ernest Allen, "Keeping Children Safe: Rhetoric and Reality," *Juv. Just.* (May 1998): 16–17 (indicating that a person trying to ensnare a child will attempt to seem caring, persuasive, and non-threatening in order to overcome the label of being a "stranger").

16. A. Kent, "The Reality of the Nightmare," *The Times*, August 15, 1990, quoted in Allen, "Keeping Children Safe," 16–17.

17. See, e.g., Mikell v. State, 637 S.E.2d 142, 145-46 (Ga. Ct. App. 2006) (outlining how a six-year-old child agreed to follow a stranger molester to the second floor of her home where she was molested).

18. Kenneth V. Lanning, *Child Molesters: A Behavioral Analysis*, 5th ed. (National Center. for Missing and Exploited Children, 2011), 8.

19. Ryan C. W. Hall & Richard C. W. Hall, "A Profile of Pedophilia: Definition, Characteristics of Offenders, Recidivism, Treatment Outcomes, and Forensic Issues," *Mayo Clinic Proc.* 82, no. 4, (2007): 461.

20. Lanning, *Child Molesters*, 8.

21. See Roland C. Summit, "The Child Sexual Abuse Accommodation Syndrome," *Child Abuse & Neglect* 7 (1983): 177, 182.

22. Hall and Hall, "A Profile of Pedophilia," 461.

23. Salter, *Predators*, 45.

24. See, e.g., State v. Jacobson, 930 A.2d 628, 635-36 (Conn. 2006) (describing the grooming stages).

25. Lanning, *Child Molesters*, 38.

26. Salter, *Predator*, 42.

27. Ibid.

28. See, e.g., Oliver v. State, 977 So. 2d 673, 676 (Fla. Dist. Ct. App. 2008) (describing how the defendant was "[a]lmost like a father figure" because of the attention he showered upon the victim, gaining the child's trust and confidence).

29. See, e.g., State v. DeVincentis, 74 P.3d 119, 125 (Wash. 2003) (en banc) (discussing the defendant's "scheme" to befriend children through his own daughter, which brought children into his home, providing him with the opportunity to abuse).

30. Lanning, *Child Molesters*, 27.

31. Jennifer J. Freyd, "What Juries Don't Know: Dissemination of Research on Victim Response Is Essential for Justice, Trauma" *Psychol. Newsl.* (Fall 2008): 16 ("Non-disclosure, delayed disclosure, and retraction are particularly likely in cases in which the perpetrator is close to the victim."); see also Roland C. Summit, "The Child Sexual Abuse Accommodation Syndrome," *Child Abuse & Neglect* 7 (1983): 177, 182. ("[A] child is three times more likely to be molested by a recognized, trusted adult than by a stranger."), at 182–83 ("The fact that the perpetrator is

often in a trusted and apparently loving position only increases the im-
balance of power and underscores the helplessness of the child.").

32. Salter, *Predators*, 43.

33. See, e.g., People v. Waples, 95 Cal. Rptr. 2d 45, 46–47 (Cal.
App. 2000) (stating that the defendant used his trade skills as a horse
trainer to "insinuate himself into families with young girls"); Com-
monwealth v. Ardinger, 839 A.2d 1143, 1144 (Pa. Super. Ct. 2003)
(explaining that prior to molestation, defendant became "good friends"
with child's mother who allowed him to become a "substitute father").

34. Lanning, *Child Molesters*, 72; see also Adrian v. People, 770 P.2d
1243, 1244 (Colo. 1989) (stating that the defendant was a trusted friend
of victim's family for 15 years before assaulting the victim).

35. Lanning, *Child Molesters*, 76–77.

36. See, e.g., State v. Jacobson, 930 A.2d 628, 632 (Conn. 2006)
(explaining that a youth ice hockey coach ingratiated himself into the
victim's family prior to molestation).

37. Roland C. Summit, "The Child Sexual Abuse Accommodation Syndrome," *Child Abuse & Neglect* 7 (1983): 182.

38. Lanning, *Child Molesters*, 77.

39. See generally Christa Brown, *This Little Light* (Cedarburg, WI:
Foremost Press, 2009).

40. Ibid., 14.

41. Summit, "The Child Sexual Abuse Accommodation Syndrome," 191.

42. Bette L. Bottoms, Gail S. Goodman, Beth M. Schwartz-Kenney, and Sherilyn N. Thomas, "Understanding Children's Use of Secrecy in the Context of Eyewitness Reports," *Law & Hum. Behav.* 26
(2002): 285, 306.

43. Ibid., 287.

44. Lanning, *Child Molesters*, 58.

45. See, e.g., People v. Watson, 281 A.D.2d 691, 697 (N.Y. App.
Div. 2001) (finding that the defendant's physical abuse of family members created sufficient control to sexually molest a fourteen- or fifteen-
year-old); Sands v. State, 662 S.E.2d 374, 375 (Ga. Ct. App. 2008)
(reciting the facts that the defendant placed child's hands on his penis
and also inserted his penis into her vagina).

46. Lanning, *Child Molesters*, 9 (noting the exception of acquaintance molestation related to child prostitution). Another exception is that physical force is more commonly used by juvenile sexual offenders—over one-third of juvenile sex offenses involve some form of physical force. Victor Vieth, "When the Child Abuser is a Child: Investigating, Prosecuting and Treating Juvenile Sex Offenders in the New Millennium," Hamline L. Rev. (2001): 47, 51. Adolescent offenders are also more likely to employ force or threats as a means of keeping the victim silent after the abuse is completed. Id. This is often because the "immaturity, lower cognitive ability, and closeness in age to the victim may make it more difficult for the juvenile offender to entice the victim with gifts and desensitization efforts."

47. Lanning, *Child Molesters*, 10.

48. See, e.g., People v. West, 2008 Cal. App. LEXIS 2865, at *4 (Cal. Ct. App. April 7, 2008) ("When [the child] did not comply with defendant's sexual requests, defendant would yell at [the child] and get physically violent (emphasis added)); Murphy v. Merzbacher, 697 A.2d 861, 863 (Md. 1997) (reciting the fact that an acquaintance molester threatened each victim with physical violence if they reported the abuse).

49. Donald G. Fischer, and Wendy L. McDonald, "Characteristics of Intrafamilial and Extrafamilial Child Sexual Abuse," *Child Abuse & Neglect* 22 (1998): 915.

50. Lanning, *Child Molesters*, 9; see also State v. Rawls, 649 So.2d 1350, 1353 (Fla. 1994) (describing a broadly defined familial relationship to be one in which there is a "recognizable bond of trust with the defendant, similar to the bond that develops between a child and her grandfather, uncle, or guardian").

51. Gene G. Abel & Nora Harlow, "The Abel and Harlow Child Molestation Prevention Study," in *The Stop Child Molestation Book* (2001), 8; see also Finkelhor, *Sourcebook on Child Sexual Abuse* (1986), 21 (documenting a survey finding that family members were responsible for perpetrating sexual abuse upon 29% of all minor females who have been sexually victimized. Of those victims, 6% were abused by a father or stepfather).

52. Biological and step-parents usually reside within the same home as the victim, while more distant relatives are often granted access simply because they are a relative. See State v. Merida, 960 A.2d 228, 231 (R.I.

2008) (describing a granddaughter being molested repeatedly by her grandfather while she routinely spent weekends with her grandparents).

53. Fischer, and McDonald, "Characteristics of Intrafamilial and Extrafamilial Child Sexual Abuse," 925.

54. Lanning, *Child Molesters*, 9.

55. See State v. Etheridge, 352 S.E.2d 673, 681 (N.C. 1987) (opining in dicta that "[t]he youth and vulnerability of children, coupled with the power inherent in a parent's position of authority, creates a unique situation of dominance and control. . . .").

56. Lanning, *Child Molesters*, 9.

57. Ibid., 10. Such basic necessities include food, clothing, shelter, and attention.

58. See, e.g., Ledbetter v. State, 129 P.3d 671, 675 (Nev. 2006) (reciting the facts that the stepfather warned the child victim that if she disclosed the abuse, he would go to prison and she would be acting selfishly and would break up the family).

59. Diane Mandt Langberg, *On the Threshold of Hope* (Carol Stream, IL: Tyndale House, 1999), 113.

60. John B. Murray, "Psychological Profile of Pedophiles and Child Molesters," *J. Psychol.* 134 (2000): 211, 214.

61. See, e.g., State v. J.M., 941 So.2d. 686, 691 (La. Ct. App. 2006) (describing how a ten-year-old victim's grandfather made her play "Doctor" in his greenhouse and made her watch a "dirty movie"); People v. Wardlaw, 794 N.Y.S.2d 524, 526 (N.Y. App. Div. 2005) (stating that victim "did as she was told" when molested by her half-uncle).

62. Fischer & McDonald, "Characteristics of Intrafamilial and Extrafamilial Child Sexual Abuse," 917. ("Duration of abuse has generally been found to be greater for intrafamilial than extrafamilial sexual abuse. This has been attributed to the greater accessibility of victims in interfamilial cases . . . and the lower likelihood of reporting, or reporting early, sexual abuse in intrafamilial cases.")

63. Tina B. Goodman-Brown et al., "Why Children Tell: A Model of Children's Disclosure of Sexual Abuse," *Child Abuse & Neglect* 27 (2003): 525, 526.

64. Ibid., 536.

65. Soper v. State, 731 P.2d 587, 588 (Alaska Ct. App. 1987).

66.   Jennifer J. Freyd, "Violations of Power, Adaptive Blindness and Betrayal Trauma Theory," *Feminism & Psychol.* 7 (1997): 22, 26.

67.   Ibid., 28. Dr. Freyd has also found that the closeness of victim and perpetrator is related to the probability that the child will have some degree of amnesia regarding the childhood sexual abuse.

68.   A 1998 study found intra-familial abusers instruct their victims more often than acquaintance molesters to remain silent about the abuse. See Fischer & McDonald, "Characteristics of Intrafamilial and Extrafamilial Child Sexual Abuse," 928.

69.   Bette L. Bottoms, Gail S. Goodman, Beth M. Schwartz-Kenney, and Sherilyn N. Thomas, "Understanding Children's Use of Secrecy in the Context of Eyewitness Reports," *Law & Hum. Behav.* 26 (2002): 291.

70.   Robert Dubé & Martine Hébert, "Sexual Abuse of Children Under 12 Years of Age: A Review of 511 Cases," *Child Abuse & Neglect* 12 (1998): 327.

71.   Fischer & McDonald, "Characteristics of Intrafamilial and Extrafamilial Child Sexual Abuse," 927.

72.   Lana Stermac, Kathryn Hall, and Marianne Henskens, "Violence Among Child Molesters," *J. Sex Res.* 26 (1989): 453; see also State v. Merida, 960 A.2d 228, 231 (R.I. 2008) (reciting the fact that the defendant "grabbed and held onto" nine-year-old's breasts while also touching the inside of her privates with his fingers); Ledbetter v. State, 129 P.3d 671, 675 (Nev. 2006) (reciting the fact that a six-year-old woke in pain to find her step-father inserting his fingers inside of her vagina).

73.   Lana Stermac, Kathryn Hall, and Marianne Henskens, "Violence Among Child Molesters," *J. Sex Res.* 26 (1989): 927.

74.   See, e.g., United States v. Hawpetoss, 478 F.3d 820, 822 (7th Cir. 2007) (noting testimony that the defendant sexually assaulted his fourteen-year-old stepdaughter at knifepoint).

75.   See Benjamin P. Matthews & Donald C. Bross, "Mandated Reporting Is Still a Policy with Reason: Empirical Evidence and Philosophical Grounds," *Child Abuse & Neglect* 32 (2008): 511, 512 (noting that in 2004, children were the direct source of their own referral in only 0.5% of all substantiated abuse cases); see also, Payne v. State, 674 S.E.2d 298, 299 (Ga. 2009) (reciting testimony that the defendant held down his

eleven-year-old stepdaughter and "threatened her with physical harm");
State v. Weatherbee, 762 P.2d 590, 591 (Ariz. Ct. App. 1988) (stating
that the defendant threatened to hurt his sixteen-year-old daughter with
his pistol if she "told anyone about the sexual abuse").

Policy Section Two

1. A. F. Lieberman, and P. Van Horn, *Psychotherapy with Infants
and Young Children: Repairing the Effects of Stress and Trauma on Early
Attachment* (New York: The Guilford Press, 2008).

Chapter Five

1. Anna Salter, *Predators, Pedophiles, Rapists, and Other Sex Offenders: Who They Are, How They Operate, and How We Can Protect Ourselves and Our Children* (New York: Basic Books, 2003), 229.

2. For an excellent overview of hiring practices that should be incorporated into the Policy, see J. Saul, and N. C. Audage, (2007). *Preventing Child Sexual Abuse within Youth-Serving Organizations: Getting
Started on Policies and Procedures* (Washington, DC: U.S. Department
of Health and Human Services, Centers for Disease Control and Prevention, National Center for Injury Prevention and Control, Division
of Violence Prevention, 2007), 4, retrieved from www.cdc.gov/violen-
ceprevention/pdf/PreventingChildSexualAbuse-a.pdf#page=1.

3. Gavin de Becker, *Gift of Fear: Survival Signals that Protect Us
From Violence* (New York: Dell Publishing, 1997), 70.

4. Privacy Rights Clearinghouse (2016), "Volunteer background
checks: giving back without giving up on privacy," retrieved from
www.privacyrights.org/volunteer-background-checks-without-giving-
up-privacy.

5. An example of this phenomenon can be found in a November
2016 response to a Freedom of Information Law (FOIL) request submitted by attorney Elliot Pasik to the New York State Education Department. According to the response, 2,572 public school district job
applicants (not including New York City) were denied employment
since 2001 due to their criminal history. To view a copy of the Department's FOIL response, contact GRACE.

6. C. J. Sugayan, *Coverage and Liability Issues in Sexual Misconduct
Claims* (Princeton, NJ: Munich Re-insurance America, Inc., 2005).

7. An arrest record can be helpful information in that many criminal cases are resolved when the prosecutor allows the defendant to enter a plea to a reduced and/or less serious charge. Having knowledge of the charge that was the basis of the arrest can be very helpful when assessing whether an individual is qualified to serve.

8. Even when a child abuser is caught and successfully prosecuted, the crime still may not appear on a criminal background check if the offender was a juvenile when the offense was committed, if the record was expunged or sealed, or if a clerical error was made.

9. Gavin de Becker, *Gift of Fear: Survival Signals that Protect Us From Violence* (New York: Dell Publishing, 1997), 158.

10. Numerous states have anti-discrimination laws, which make it illegal to ask applicants and references whether the applicants were ever arrested or charged with abusing children. In some jurisdictions, like New York City, employers are additionally prohibited from inquiring about convictions, until they have extended a conditional offer to the applicant. However, even in these jurisdictions, it is legal to ask about an applicant's ideas and behaviors. If a reference is only answering the most factual of questions, inquire whether the limited response is a reflection on the applicant or the result of that organization's policy. If the latter, try finding a replacement reference—possibly even by asking the reticent reference to recommend another reference outside of that organization.

11. See S. South, A. Shlonsky, R. Mildon, A. Pourliakas, J. Falkiner, and A. Laughlin, *Scoping Review: Evaluations of Pre-employment Screening Practices for Child-Related Work that Aim to Prevent Child Sexual Abuse* (Melbourne, Australia: Parenting Research Centre and the University of Melbourne, 2015), 42, retrieved from www.childabuse-royalcommission.gov.au/getattachment/3828bdcb-3689-4011-98a3-d2ebbf277718/Evaluations-of-pre-employment-screening-practices.

12. For additional sample reference questions, see: Appendix 3 of TBI's policy: Temple Beth Israel, *Safeguarding Our Children Policy: Code of Conduct* (2015), retrieved from www.tbi.org.au/wp-content/uploads/2016/06/Safeguarding-our-Children-Policy-FINAL.pdf.

13. Bear in mind though, that no matter how intent you are on keeping children safe, there are legal and moral limits to what you may ask. Ensure that at all times you keep questions professional, and never ask an applicant discriminatory (about ethnic descent), invasive

(do you plan on becoming pregnant soon?), or harassing (are you currently dating?) questions. It is advisable to meet with an employment attorney in your state when drafting Policy language and sample questions, so that you can ensure compliance with local and federal laws.

14. For additional sample interview questions, see Appendix 2 of TBI's policy: Temple Beth Israel, *Safeguarding Our Children Policy: Code of Conduct* (2015), retrieved from: www.tbi.org.au/wp-content/uploads/2016/06/Safeguarding-our-Children-Policy-FINAL.pdf or Appendix 6 of Leibler Yavneh College, *Child Protection Policy: Prevention—Detection—Responding* (2016), retrieved from http://www.yavneh.vic.edu.au/wp-content/uploads/2016/05/Child_Protection_Policy.pdf.

15. Salter, *Predators*, 202: "You are never going to run into a child molester who is not a practiced liar, even if he is not a natural one."

16. B. DePaulo, "Why are we so bad at detecting lies?" www.psychologytoday.com, May, 2013, retrieved from www.psychologytoday.com/blog/living-single/201305/why-are-we-so-bad-detecting-lies; Salter, *Predators*, 40, 161–163.

17. Saul and Audage, *Preventing Child Sexual Abuse within Youth-Serving Organizations: Getting Started on Policies and Procedures*, 4, retrieved from www.cdc.gov/violenceprevention/pdf/PreventingChild-SexualAbuse-a.pdf#page=1.

Chapter Six

1. D. Finkelhor, R. Omrod, and M. Chaffin, *Juveniles Who Commit Sex Offenses Against Minors* (Juvenile Justice Bulletin, Office of Juvenile Justice & Delinquency Prevention, 2009), retrieved from www.ncjrs.gov/pdffiles1/ojjdp/227763.pdf.

2. In this study of adult offenders, 24 percent also reported sexually abusing a child when another adult was present, and 14 percent reported molesting a child when both another child and another adult were present. Of those who had not abused a child in the presence of others, 64 percent believed they may have progressed to that point had they not been arrested and placed in treatment. See R. C. Underwood, P. C. Patch, G. C. Cappelletty, and R. W. Wolfe, (1999). "Do Sexual Offenders Molest When Other People Are Present? A Preliminary Investigation," *Sexual Abuse: A Journal of Research and Treatment* 11 (1999): 243–47.

3. For factors that contribute to a child's risk of being sexually abused, including family structure, age, and location, see: A. J. Sedlak, J. Mettenburg, M. Basena, I. Petta, K. McPherson, A. Greene, and S. Li, *Fourth National Incidence Study of Child Abuse and Neglect (NIS–4): Report to Congress* (Washington, DC: U.S. Department of Health and Human Services, Administration for Children and Families, 2010), retrieved from www.acf.hhs.gov/sites/default/files/opre/nis4_report_congress_full_pdf_jan2010.pdf.

4. While legally churches need only obtain permission from caregivers and not children, receiving permission from children who are old enough to give it sends a strong message of respect for their wishes regarding their own privacy; this is a critical theme in countering child abuse.

Chapter Seven

1. Churches may wish to consult with their insurance company or lawyer in determining this age.

2. A decision to leave doors open must be weighed against the risk of a child running out or stragglers wandering in.

Policy Section Three

1. J. Stark, "How to Protect Your Workplace against Child Abuse," *The Sunday Morning Herald*, September 12, 2014, retrieved from www.smh.com.au/national/how-to-protect-your-workplace-against-child-abuse-20140912-10g289.html.

Chapter Eight

1. Stark, "How to Protect Your Workplace against Child Abuse," retrieved from www.smh.com.au/national/how-to-protect-your-workplace-against-child-abuse-20140912-10g289.html.

Chapter Ten

1. This is especially true for incest cases, where in one study child molesters who sexually abused children in their families reported committing on average 45.2 acts of sexual abuse against one girl victim and 36.5 acts of sexual abuse against one boy victim. See: G. G. Abel, J. V. Becker, M. Mittelman, J. Cunningham-Rathner, J. L. Rouleau, and W.

D. Murphy, "Self-Reported Sex Crimes of Nonincarcerated Paraphiliacs," *Journal of Interpersonal Violence* 2 (1987): 3–25.

2. V. I. Vieth, "When Days Are Gray: Avoiding Burnout as Child Abuse Professionals," Update, 14, Alexandria, VA: National District Attorney's Association: National Center for Prosecution of Child Abuse, 2001.

3. J. Drape, "Penn State to Pay Nearly $60 Million to 26 Abuse Victims," *New York Times*, October 29, 2013, retrieved from www.nytimes.com/2013/10/29/sports/ncaafootball/penn-state-to-pay-59-7-million-to-26-sandusky-victims.html?_r=0. An independent investigation discovered a "total disregard for the safety and welfare" of child victims. See: L. Freeh, "Remarks of Louis Freeh in Conjunction with Announcement of Publication of Report Regarding the Pennsylvania State University," (2012), retrieved from www.prnewswire.com/news-releases/remarks-of-louis-freeh-in-conjunction-with-announcement-of-publication-of-report-regarding-the-pennsylvania-state-university-162194405.html.

4. J. Drape, "Sandusky Guilty of Sexual Abuse of 10 Young Boys," *New York Times*, June 23, 2012, retrieved from www.nytimes.com/2012/06/23/sports/ncaafootball/jerry-sandusky-convicted-of-sexually-abusing-boys.html?_r=1&.

5. For an excellent discussion of the problem and a straightforward solution, see V. I. Vieth, et al., "Lessons from Penn State: A call to implement a new pattern of training for mandated reporters and child protection professionals," *CenterPiece* 3 (2012): 1–10, retrieved from www.gundersenhealth.org/app/files/public/1436/CenterPiece-Vol-3-Issue-3-4.pdf.

6. The criterion of "reasonable cause to suspect" is provided by New York Soc. Serv. Law § 413 and 414. Other states may have different criteria for reporting. See the Child Welfare Information Gateway, "Mandatory Reporters of Child Abuse and Neglect," US Department of Health and Human Services (2015), retrieved from www.childwelfare.gov/pubPDFs/manda.pdf.

7. A telephone interview of 2,000 children in the mid-1990s revealed that only 6 percent of children who had been victims of attempted or completed sexual abuse had reported the abuse to an authority figure of any type. See: D. Finkelhor, and J. Dziuba-Leatherman, (1994). "Children as Victims of Violence: A National Survey," *Pediatrics* 94 (1994): 413–20.

Chapter Eleven

1. If your church has any concerns over whether an independent review is appropriate, contact your GRACE Certification specialist or similar child protection expert.

2. Reports that fall under the first category will almost always require some form of independent investigatory review. Different churches will have different financial situations, and some churches will not be able to afford a formal investigatory review. The consultation with the oversight organization will determine viable options in addressing any of the three circumstances where some form of independent review is needed.

3. The investigator will be a current or former child abuse prosecutor or law enforcement officer with significant experience in handling cases of maltreatment. Depending upon the nature of the review and available resources, the oversight organization may also seek the consultation of a mental health professional, pastor, or other professional that may be needed. The need for more multi-disciplined assistance will be determined on a case-by-case basis.

4. There are numerous organizations that meet this standard. These organizations include GRACE, the National Center for Prosecution of Child Abuse, the National Center for Missing & Exploited Children, the National Child Protection Training Center, Fox Valley Technical College, and the American Professional Society on the Abuse of Children.

5. See generally, Victor I. Vieth, "Unto the Third Generation: A Call to End Child Abuse in the United States within 120 Years" (Revised and Expanded) *Hamline Journal of Law and Public Policy* 28, no. 3 (2006); Kelly M. Champion, Kimberly Shipman, Barbara L. Bonner, Lisa Hensley, and Allison C. Howe, "Child Maltreatment Training in Doctoral Programs in Clinical, Counseling, and School Psychology: Where Do We Go From Here?" *Child Maltreatment* 8 (August, 2003): 211, 215; Ann S. Botash, M.D., "From Curriculum to Practice: Implementation of the Child Abuse Curriculum," *Child Maltreatment* 8 (November 2003): 239; Jenny et. al, "Analysis of Missed Cases of Abusive Head Trauma," *Jama* 281 (1999): 621–26; Robert H. McCormick, "The Master of Arts in Child Advocacy: A Contribution to an Emerging Discipline," *Journal of Aggression, Maltreatment & Trauma* 12 (2006): 149; Suzanne P. Starling,

and Stephen Boos, "Core Content for Residency Training in Child Abuse and Neglect," *Child Maltreatment* 8, no. 4 (November, 2003): 242–43.

Policy Section Four

1. V. I. Veith, D. F. W. Tchividjian, and K. R. Knodel, K.R. (2012). "Child Abuse and the Church: a Call for Prevention, Treatment and Training," *Journal of Psychology and Theology* 40 (2012): 323–30. See generally, T. Bryant-Davis, M. U. Ellis, E. Burke-Maynard, N. Moon, P. A. Counts, and G. Anderson, "Religiosity, Spirituality, and Trauma Recovery in the Lives of Children and Adolescents," *Professional Psychology: Research & Practice* 43 (2012): 306–14; D. F. Walker, H. W. Reid, T. O'Neil, and L. Brown, "Changes in Personal Religion/Spirituality during and after Childhood Abuse: A Review and Synthesis," *Psychological Trauma Theory Research Practice and Policy* 1 (2009): 130–45; Elliott, D. M. (1994). T. L. Gall, V. Basque, M. Damasceno-Scott, and G. Vardy, (2007). "Spirituality and the Current Adjustment of Adult Survivors of Childhood Sexual Abuse," *Journal for the Scientific Study of Religion* 46 (2007): 101–17.

2. B. Tchividjian, "Heroes in Our Midst: Chris Anderson & Male Survivor (Part II)," Religion News Service, October 31, 2014, retrieved from http://boz.religionnews.com/2014/10/31/heroes-midst-chris-anderson-malesurvivor-part-ii/#sthash.zEInMzlV.dpuf.

3. V. I. Vieth, M. D. Everson, V. Vaughan-Eden, and S. Tiapula, "Chaplains for Children: Twelve Potential Roles for a Theologian on the MDT," *CenterPiece* 3, no. 6, 1–5, retrieved from http://www.gundersenhealth.org/app/files/public/1438/CenterPiece-Vol-3-Issue-6.pdf.

Chapter Twelve

1. This chapter outlines recommendations for supporting the child or adult survivor. None of these recommendations stand alone; all are meant to be read in conjunction with recommendations in other chapters about intervening to protect the child and reporting suspicions of abuse.

2. In a study of 116 cases of confirmed sexual abuse, almost 80 percent of the children initially denied the abuse or tentatively disclosed, 75 percent of those who disclosed did so by accident, and over 20 percent of the children ultimately recanted their disclosure, even though the abuse had occurred. See: T. Sorensen, and B. Snow, "How Children Tell: The Process of Disclosure in Child Sexual Abuse," *Child Welfare League of*

America 70 (1991): 3–15. See also L. Lawson, and M. Chaffin, (1992). "False Negatives in Sexual Abuse Disclosure Interviews," *Journal of Interpersonal Violence* 7 (1992): 532–542; and Section 5.1, especially footnote 1, of the John Jay Report: John Jay College of Criminal Justice, City University of New York (2004). The nature and scope of sexual abuse of minors by Catholic priests and deacons in the United States 1950–2002. United States Conference of Catholic Bishops. Retrieved from www.bishop-accountability.org/reports/2004_02_27_JohnJay_revised/2004_02_27_John_Jay_Main_Report_Optimized.pdf.

3. F. McClure, D. V. Chavez, M. D. Agars, M. J. Peacock, and A. Matosian, "Resilience in Sexually Abused Women: Risk and Protective Factors," *Journal of Family Violence* 23 (2008): 81–88; G. Horner, "Child Sexual Abuse: Consequences and Implications," *Journal of Pediatric Health Care* 24 (2009): 358–64; C. Tremblay, M. Hebert, and C. Piche, "Coping Strategies and Social Support as Mediators of Consequences in Child Sexual Abuse Victims," *Child Abuse & Neglect* 23 (1999): 929–45; E. L. Kinnally, Y. Huang, R. Haverly, A. K. Burke, H. Galfalvy, D. P. Brent, J. J. Mann, "Parental Care Moderates the Influence of MAOA-uVNTR Genotype and Childhood Stressors on Trait Impulsivity and Aggression in Adult Women," *Psychiatric Genetics* 19 (2009): 126–33.

4. Anna Salter, *Predators, Pedophiles, Rapists, and Other Sex Offenders: Who They Are, How They Operate, and How We Can Protect Ourselves and Our Children* (New York: Basic Books, 2003), 14.

5. J. Cashmore, A. Taylor, R. Shackel, and P. Parkinson, 2016, "The Impact of Delayed Reporting on the Prosecution and Outcomes of Child Sexual Abuse Cases," Royal Commission into Institutional Responses to Child Sexual Abuse, Sydney (2016), retrieved from www.childabuseroyalcommission.gov.au/policy-and-research/our-research/published-research/the-impact-of-delayed-reporting-on-the-prosecution.

6. Tchividjian, "Heroes in Our Midst: Chris Anderson & MaleSurvivor (Part II)," retrieved from http://boz.religionnews.com/2014/10/31/heroes-midst-chris-anderson-malesurvivor-part-ii/#sthash.zEInMzlV.dpuf.

7. Ibid.

8. J. Shore, "6 Truths about Forgiving Sexual Abuse," Patheos, November 6, 2014, retrieved from www.patheos.com/blogs/johnshore/2014/11/6-truths-about-forgiving-sexual-abuse/#ixzz3PzUeWoEu.

9. Ibid.

10. This list has been adapted from J. S. Holcomb, L. A. Holcomb, *Rid of My Disgrace: Hope and Healing for Victims of Sexual Assault* (Wheaton, IL: Crossway, 2011). See excerpt at www.netgrace.org/resources/2015/4/9/what-to-say-and-what-not-to-say-to-a-victim-of-sexual-assault.

Chapter Thirteen

1. A. Weiss, *Principles of Spiritual Activism* (New York: Ktav Publishing House Inc., 2002), 138.

2. These steps are in addition to the steps outlined in Chapter Ten, "Reporting."

3. In most cases, the Support Person will reach out to the child and the child's family. However, in some instances, it may be appropriate to reach out and offer support only to the child (e.g., a teenager who has been abused by both parents), while abiding by the *Interaction Guidelines* outlined in this Policy.

4. Victor Vieth, "Is It Safe to Go Back to Church?" *Boundless* (2014), retrieved from www.boundless.org/relationships/2014/is-it-safe-to-go-back-to-church.

5. Ibid.

6. See South Carolina's *Silent Tears* report for training recommendations. Gunderson National Child Protection Training Center, *Silent Tears—The View from the Trenches: Recommendations for Improving South Carolina's Response to Child Sexual Abuse Based on Insight from Frontline Child Protection Professionals*, (2013), 78, retrieved from www.gundersenhealth.org/app/files/public/2773/NCPTC-Silent-Tears-final-report.pdf.

7. These steps are in addition to the steps outlined above in "Policy Violations" and "Reporting" to protect abused children from further abuse.

8. In most cases, the Support Person will reach out to the child and the child's family. However, in some instances it may be appropriate to reach out and offer support only to the child (e.g., a teenager who has been abused by both parents), while abiding by the "Safe Behaviors" outlined in this Policy.

Appendix Two

1. Adapted from Church Pension Group, "Model Policies for the Protection of Children and Youth from Abuse, " retrieved from https://www.

cpg.org/linkservid/3F743B4C-06F1-5DFF-86FFB64C8B79DE07/
showMeta/0/?label=Model%20Policies%3A%20Preventing%20Chil-
dren%20and%20Youth%20from%20Abuse and Victor Vieth's consultation to Greta. Your church should confirm with an employment attorney that this form complies with state and local laws.

Appendix Three

1. In one study, convicted child molesters were asked to advise caregivers on how they could better protect their children. One offender
advised caregivers to educate their children about sex and sexual abuse
stating "caregivers . . . (who) don't tell their children about these things
(sexual matters)—I used it to my advantage by teaching the child myself." For details on other responses given, see: M. Elliot, K. Browne,
and J. Kilcoyne, "Child Sexual Abuse Prevention: What Offenders Tell
Us," *Child Abuse & Neglect* 5 (1995): 579–94.

2. Educate2Empower Publishing has additional signs available
for download and freely available to share at http://somesecrets.info/
posters/.

3. Caregivers and educators should avoid the terms "good-touch"
and "bad touch," because abusive touch can sometimes feel like "good
touch." Moreover, the term "bad touch" is laden with judgment. If children become the victim of abuse, they may believe that they have done
something bad, and will be reluctant to tell. Alternatively, a children may
understand "bad touch" to mean that the person who touched them
is bad, and may be reluctant to "tattletale," particularly if the abuser is
someone the child loves, a caregiver, or respected member of the community.